THE
CONSERVATORY
BOOK

THE CONSERVATORY BOOK

Peter Marston

CASSELL&CO

First published in the United Kingdom in 2001 by Cassell & Co
Text copyright © Peter Marston
Design and layout copyright © Cassell & Co

Photographs by Peter Marston and John Heseltine
The photographic acknowledgements on page 160 constitute an extension to this
copyright page.

A CIP catalogue record for this book is available from the British Library.

Editor Catherine Bradley
Text editor Judy Spours
Indexer Drusilla Calvert

Design Director David Rowley
Designed by Nigel Soper

ISBN 0 304 35638 7

Catalogues for Marston & Langinger conservatories and garden room furnishings
may be ordered, telephone +44 (0) 207 823 6829 (USA: 212 575 0554).
Or visit the website: http://www.marston-and-langinger.com

Typeset in Arepo and Interstate
Printed and bound in Italy by Printer Trento S.r.l.

Cassell & Co, Wellington House, 125 Strand,
London WC2R OBB

Introduction

When I wrote my first book on this subject ten years ago, many people were unfamiliar with conservatories. They were just coming back into vogue after a seventy-year absence and I still sometimes had to explain that, by a conservatory, I didn't mean a music school. There has since been a dramatic rise in their popularity: nowadays conservatories are seen as an easy way of extending the home, making the most of an unusual or difficult area. However, their unique, exciting and essentially modernist architecture is not always understood, nor their contemporary possibilities fully recognized. This new book explores the special contribution of the conservatory to an informal home style, suited to the way we lead our lives.

All conservatories, of whatever size, share an appreciation of the outdoors from inside. While early examples were built to protect tender plants from a harsher exterior climate, contemporary conservatories more often provide a comfortable room for year-round enjoyment of the surrounding garden. With their high glass roofs and large windows, and doors opening on to the terrace, conservatories create a special environment that is stylish and practical, different from the rest of the house.

Variously called orangery, garden room, winter garden, sun-room or veranda, the conservatory has now developed a style distinct from its historical predecessors. Relatively recent developments in glass have produced double-glazing that is secure, warm in winter and able to control the impact of summer sunlight. Combined with effective heating and ventilation, these qualities make the conservatory a versatile house extension, linking existing rooms and the garden without loss of light. Released from the limitations of the greenhouse, the conservatory can now function as dining room, studio or kitchen, or it can even contain an entire home. Thoughtfully designed and well built, a conservatory can add to the architecture of the house, and make a lasting investment.

In this book I explain the different types and styles of conservatory, the practicalities of building one and how to determine its most appropriate shape, location and look. I consider the role of the surrounding garden and terrace, and discuss the choice of furniture, plants and decoration for the interior design. I hope you will be inspired, as I have been, by the excitement of living under glass.

PETER MARSTON
LONDON
JANUARY 2001

Contents

1

The Role of the Conservatory

Once a glazed horticultural building to preserve delicate plants, the contemporary conservatory has become a part of the home. Set between house and terrace, it provides a light, flexible space that recent technology has made safe, comfortable and suitable for year-round use. Modern conservatory architecture and interior design often respect and draw on features, colours and materials of the surrounding gardens and buildings. Many also reflect the ingenuity and diversity of traditional plant houses – classical orangeries, cast-iron crystal palaces and exuberant nineteenth-century conservatories. Their bold style and decoration can be successfully reinterpreted for contemporary needs. The conservatory can provide valuable additional space that enhances rather than detracts from the existing architecture, whether country cottage or city roof-top home.

Size, Shape and Location

Throughout this book, I stress the importance of individuality, of constructing and decorating buildings to serve their owners' needs and tastes while respecting the style and proportion of adjacent buildings. Since I designed and built my first glasshouses, a host of companies have sprung up, offering standard patterns or modular systems of components which rarely meet these design criteria. It is important to increase the height and scale with the length, or thicken the framework in scale with the size, so that the conservatory will look and feel right and sit comfortably alongside an existing building.

If you are commissioning a conservatory, first decide how it will be used. Are you seeking extra space or a different kind of space? Does your home lack light or a large room for entertaining? Could access to the garden be improved by linking it to the house? Will you eat in the conservatory, in which case how big a table will be needed and for how many? Do you want to grow plants or to relax with a view of the garden? Does the house have an awkward outside area which a conservatory addition could resolve, adding value by improving the look and shape of the building?

The designer or architect should first ask you about these points, listening to your ideas and likes or dislikes, and then discuss the practical issues. These should take account of your budget, how the addition can be joined and assimilated into the existing architecture, and the complexities of obtaining permission. Expect first to see a sketch design, rather than technical drawings, showing the style and proportion of the scheme, with sufficient of the surroundings shown to give a true impression of the building's scale and impact. Good perspective drawings are a great help, but they should be accompanied or followed by accurately scaled drawings indicating every side of the construction, to enable you to assess the worst as well as the best aspects of the proposal. Meet the designer to discuss the drawings (postal design is much less likely to succeed), and if the first sketches are not what you had in mind, and provided you have a rapport with the designer, ask for more. After all, their purpose is to avoid costly changes when construction has started. It is only possible to obtain an accurate costing after the design and specifications are agreed; in fact, a fixed price offered earlier should cause concern.

Above: By using a steep pitch, the roof and sides are combined in this stylized modern building. This design approach depends on air conditioning and solar-controlled glass, but the overall effect is stunning.

Left: I used an orangery style as the centrepiece of a garden I designed in 1995 for a mellow, eighteenth-century Surrey rectory. The wings house an exercise room, showers and changing rooms, and the orangery was designed for use in conjunction with an outside pool and terrace.

Right: An octagonal conservatory is set in a garden and surrounded by trees. It is linked to the house by a glazed corridor (just visible on the right). In the centre of the building is a towering palm tree.

Placing the conservatory

Introducing a conservatory on to a house impacts on the inside as well as the outside, and can change the interior space and light significantly. There are a variety of design solutions for different situations.

The obvious advantage of glass construction is that the natural light in the rooms behind the extension increases. Most are built with single or pairs of glazed doors (preferably folding back) into the conservatory, but it is worth considering a larger opening or even removing the entire dividing wall to make a single, dramatically large room. This will need the advice of a structural engineer, but will be feasible in terms of insulation and security if the right construction, glass and security fittings are used. Such a solution will open up the interior of the house, and is especially effective when the conservatory adjoins the kitchen or family

room. As part of a large extension, or on a tiny house, this arrangement can be incorporated into the general layout to create bright, contemporary space even in what may externally be a traditional style.

When building against the exterior wall of a house, windows are often converted into doorways relatively easily, especially if the existing arch or lintel can be retained. Some of their logic is lost if existing windows are covered by a conservatory, and it is often more satisfactory to block them up and have large glazed doors to admit light and air from the conservatory into the room behind. It is not always feasible to build a conservatory against the wall of a house if it has low eaves. For a period house which has a formal, symmetrical design, a solution is to set the conservatory apart with a link that is glazed on at least one side. This can be either a corridor with a flat, solid roof or a

Above: This charming retreat, set in a wooded English garden, is remote from the house and can only be reached via a ladder. However, it is light, comfortable and has views on every side.

'A conservatory can be a new living space attached to the house or a peaceful retreat amongst trees in the garden.'

narrow conservatory structure. Unfettered by the constraints of building it on to the house, the conservatory can then have a bold, independent design. Links are commonly used for large conservatory poolhouses that can be out of proportion. If a house has already been extended in an awkward way, for example, or the arrangement of windows or doors is not ideal, a conservatory can cover these imperfections – assuming its location suits the internal layout and the addition improves the façade.

Confined urban locations are often about in-filling recesses between projected masonry. Although the exterior architecture is often less important, a new space, even small, can radically improve the interior. A cost-effective design for many terraced houses is to build the conservatory as a lean-to across the full width of the plot, boundary wall to boundary wall. Although these may need raising up, the conservatory will make a big new space and can be used to link the rooms behind. Bear in mind if you are planning an urban conservatory that the proposal should be checked with the local Building Department at an early stage as there

are often extra restrictions in towns and cities, particularly if you are planning to build high up, on a roof top or onto the flat roof of an existing extension. Despite their small size, the impact of city conservatories, opening up and modifying the surrounding space, can be enormous.

A porch in the form of a conservatory will have a light touch. It may be built in a classical style with columns or pilasters and small-paned glazing, or reflect the pointed gables, carved brackets and coloured glass of nineteenth-century designs. The typical arrangement has a central, inward-opening door leading towards the main house door, a broad bench running down each side and a central hanging lantern. Apart from insulating entrance and hallway, a porch can be useful architecturally, to enliven a plain façade or to shift the visual emphasis from another part of the house.

Above: A tiny city conservatory in Hampstead, London resolves an awkward recess while linking the kitchen with the garden. The Gothic glazing pattern respects the design of the eighteenth-century Gothic staircase at the rear of the house.

Left: The rural setting featured here is in fact the valleys of south Wales. The conservatory is positioned at the end of the house and introduces a formal terrace and vista punctuated with pools and paths. Looking back from the far end, the conservatory is an eye-catching element of the house.

From Orangery to Garden Room

The origins of conservatories lie in the Renaissance enthusiasm to imitate classical Italian gardens in the colder, northern European climate. This necessitated the conservation (hence 'conservatory') of tender Mediterranean plants, such as oranges and lemons, pomegranates and palms, through the winter. A simple screen to keep off frost, glazed and removable in summer, soon developed into functional glass-fronted sheds. These became the elegant, classical orangeries in the parks of great eighteenth-century houses.

At the same time, growing world trade and exploration brought new, often delicate plants from the Americas, India and Asia. The need to preserve these precious discoveries resulted in scientific study and development of glass buildings and their systems of heating and ventilation. For the first hundred years, conservatories had only a front of glass, which sufficed to keep plants alive in containers through the winter until they could be set out on terraces in spring. Attention was given to improving cultivation, so that plant specimens would flower and set seed or fruit. Stoves were used to warm the conservatory indirectly (thus avoiding the risk of poisonous fumes), and the glass

roof was invented. This dramatically increased the amount of light reaching foliage, enabling many more types of plants to be grown. As masonry or brick elements were reduced and the proportion of glass increased, the first true conservatories were created.

Orangeries

The orangery featured stone columns, a solid back wall and large, often semi-circular, sash windows (generally tall enough to walk through when open) at the sides and front. Inside would be a formal stone floor and plastered walls decorated with cornices and pilasters so that the room could be used for entertaining in summer when the over-wintered shrubs were moved out on to the terrace. Many orangeries built between the end of the seventeenth and the beginning of the nineteenth century have survived (rather better than the great iron and glass structures which followed them). Examples can be seen in stately homes throughout northern Europe and at botanical gardens, such as those in Edinburgh and at Kew in London.

Above: The combination of stone columns in-filled with painted, timber-framed, vertical glazing is attractive in this orangery at Barnsley Park in Gloucestershire, England.

Left: Constructed by conservatory builders Messenger & Co in the early 1900s as a central feature of a kitchen garden, this timber-framed conservatory has been converted for use as a home.

Right: The earliest orangeries protected plants through the winter until they could be set out in a formal but moveable garden in the spring. A rare and magnificent survivor of this style is at Versailles, outside Paris, where the orangery is built beneath the Grand Terrace.

'The delights of living under glass have transformed the conservatory from its functional beginnings to an imaginative modern space.'

window panes. Conservatories featured on the villas of the prosperous middle class, filled with exotic plants from the colonies: palms, tree ferns, begonias, orchids and aspidistras. The heady, fragrant atmosphere set the scene for afternoon tea and rubbers of bridge.

The end of an era

Towards the end of the nineteenth century, as conservatories became widespread, timber replaced iron for the framework as a more economical material, although it was usually still reinforced with iron brackets and braces. Dozens of companies competed in the conservatory market, producing brochures of steel-engraved designs which could be assembled from standardized patterns. Individuality was achieved by choosing from a repertoire of bolt-on decorations and from selections of coloured leaded lights and balconies, porches and cupolas. Conservatory design descended to dubious taste which, together with poor durability and high maintenance costs, resulted in a fall from fashion in Britain after the First World War.

Few of the smaller domestic conservatories, or the great nineteenth-century masterpieces, survived the

Left: This extraordinary Mogul glass fantasy decorates the garden of Sezincote House in Gloucestershire, England.

Right: Lucinda Lambton, photographer and architectural historian, created this vigorously Gothic conservatory for her country home.

Below: A comfortable, modern orangery is used as a lounge, complete with curtains and fully upholstered furniture.

Glasshouses of iron

By the 1800s, the growing of plants entirely under glass was widespread and well developed, but the factor determining success was still the amount of light their foliage received. Iron, first wrought, then cast, was used to make thinner and thinner glazing bars. Coupled with tiny lapped panes, usually no more than 2 mm thick, beautiful, delicate buildings were created. They grew in size to include, by the 1850s, monumental public buildings, such as the Great Palm House at Kew and the enormous Crystal Palace Exhibition Hall designed by Joseph Paxton.

The style was adapted in Britain to a domestic scale. It featured elaborate confections of glass, wood and cast iron, often richly decorated with columns and braces, finials, crestings, coloured glass and a lacework of

shortage of labour and economic crises which followed. Not until the invention of reliable double-glazing in the 1960s did the conservatory reappear.

The sun-rooms of this period were relatively simple buildings, with picture windows, low-pitched roofs and sliding doors. Ventilation and heating systems were limited and insulation was often poor, restricting the use of the space in winter or for gardening with exotic plants. In contrast to the earlier garden rooms, furnishing in these modest structures might consist of functional string matting, cane chairs and leathery house plants. Nevertheless, sun-rooms re-established the concept of recreational space linking house and garden, paving the way for the conservatories of today.

Building permission

Unlike constructions of the past, modern conservatories need to have local authority consent and to comply with building regulations. The new structure or extension should harmonize with the existing setting, and issues of size and shape should be carefully considered at the outset (see page 10). A well thought-out, coherent design that responds to specific purpose and environmental requirements is easier to justify in the application process. Standard brochure designs of fixed proportions, and height and roof pitches that

cannot be adjusted, may integrate less successfully with an intended location and be viewed less favourably by the local authority concerned.

The specific building criteria and rules vary from country to country, and even between individual counties or boroughs, but are usually based on the same principles. In order to acquire planning approval, the social, rather than personal, considerations are that the construction should not be an over-development of the site using too much green space; that the building should not be so close to the boundary that it will

Above: The painted wooden style of this modest country conservatory works well in its location, surrounded by trees.

Left: In contrast, the smart urban glitz of this conservatory in New York suits the Manhattan skyline towering above it.

Previous pages: Newly built against the timber-framed villa behind, the conservatory terraces and the room beneath flow down a hillside. The building uses both the setting and its fine views effectively.

detract from neighbouring property; and that the design and selection of building materials should be appropriate for the local style of architecture. These are generally considered using a combination of formulae, together with a review of the particular circumstances.

Building regulations must also be complied with in all cases: to ensure that buildings are safely constructed and will not collapse or spread fires; that they are properly ventilated with sufficient window space; and that they meet environmental concerns, such as being well insulated to reduce the wastage of fuel.

The criteria for permission are often more complex than you might expect. It is rarely simply a matter of following rules of thumb, such as the addition being within ten per cent of the original house's volume. Consequently, it is wise to ask advice from a local architect or surveyor able to handle the permits on your behalf. Specialist conservatory builders can also be expected to handle permits quickly and successfully as part of their service.

A further restriction arises if the conservatory is to be attached to, or is in the vicinity of, a listed, historic building. Conservation officers appreciate that historic houses are also living homes and need adapting to contemporary use, but they have the responsibility to see that alterations and additions will not detract from the original architecture. Historical features must not be damaged, and the new construction needs to be sympathetic to the old. Conservation officers usually have an enthusiastic interest in the buildings in their care and respond well to an informal discussion about proposals. They will often give useful advice about the type and design and the materials that are to be used.

It is prudent, as well as courteous, to discuss your plans in advance with interested parties. They include immediate neighbours and others who overlook, or will be overlooked, by the proposed building. Neighbours are much less likely to object if they have been shown drawings of the design and had them explained than if they simply receive an official notice of intent.

Above: An orangery-style construction is used here to create a ballroom-sized reception room alongside a large, but small-roomed, villa.

Living under Glass

With high ceilings flooding light into the interior and robust structural style, glass buildings are an exciting opportunity to create a new kitchen, family or dining room, or to introduce a study or even a poolhouse. A large conservatory can often combine different functions: for example, a garden room for eating and entertaining can incorporate a kitchen. A tiny conservatory, on the other hand, makes a perfect study; unlike a solid-walled room, its glass walls and views of the surroundings will never feel oppressive. Each of these uses imposes different practical and stylistic criteria. Success will depend on having a clear vision of how the room will be used at the earliest stage of planning. Consideration needs to be given to its size and shape, location and orientation, taking account of the activities that will take place there, the furniture that will be needed and the likely positions of openings or doors.

Opposite: Susan Hirsh designed the interior of my own small London conservatory, using a restrained palette for the walls and woodwork and pale Cotswold flags on the floor as a backdrop for the lilac, sea green and pistachio of the furniture, fabric and plants.

Using Space and Shape

In most rooms of the home it would be regarded as an inconvenience if one of the walls were out of square or the room was L-shaped; yet I am often puzzled by the irregular shape of conservatories that derive from elaborate floor plans illustrated in brochures, incorporating wrap-around features, projecting bays, extra porches and recesses. Rooms that are rectangular are generally the easiest to furnish, the exact proportions depending on the way in which they are being used. Elaborately shaped conservatories usually derive their form from a disregard of their use and a concentration instead on an impressive, multi-faceted design. Of course, there are exceptions, situations where a straightforward shape would simply look bland against, say, a Victorian villa with towers and gables. But start with the guiding principle that form should follow function – even though this is not always achieved without compromise. Many

conservatories have more doors than are ideal – openings from several rooms of the house, perhaps designed so that the garden can be reached from more than one side, or to provide lots of openings on to the terrace during the summer. The result of such multiple access can be too many routes across the conservatory and an inconvenient furniture layout. In addition, if you intend growing a collection of plants, their requirements – the amount of space and light they need – will impose on the other uses of the room, especially if it is not large.

After the first sketches of the building have been made, I recommend a tentative plan of the interior with the important elements drawn to scale: built-in fittings, shelves and storage and the larger items of furniture – tables, sofas and bigger chairs, major plants including climbers and items that will go against any solid walls. It may help if the bigger, movable items are copied on to

Left: Most of us use the conservatory as a place for informal meals close to the terrace. Protected from the weather, it is a good spot in which to relax with a view of the surrounding garden.

Right: In the spirit of a picnic, a simple meal such as breakfast can be made into an occasion. On a mild day, everything can be carried through to the conservatory and served direct from a tray.

paper or thin card, cut out and lightly stuck down, so that they can be re-positioned until everything is right. A convenient scale for the drawing is 1:20, or 1:25. It will soon become apparent whether or not the proposed conservatory – no matter how good it looks drawn in perspective – suits its intended use and is the right size and shape. I have always found that these furniture plans help resolve questions about how the space can be employed, and creative new ideas can emerge in the process. An example of this benefit occurs with the familiar bay-ended or 'octagonal' conservatory with doors at the end. A furniture plan may show that the best place for, say, a round table surrounded by chairs is in the bay end and, as a consequence, that the doors to the outside need to be moved to the side of the building.

Even if you will not be buying all the furniture immediately, and believe the room's use may change with time (good interior design should be flexible), it helps immensely to make a furniture plan to scale. At the very least, it will reveal whether the room is the right size for its intended role now and in the future; where

the doors should be; the size and quantity of furniture that it can accommodate; and what type of dining table to choose – few conservatories manage without a table for eating, entertaining, playing board games or even doing homework. Furniture plans do not need to be neat, but they must show the correct size of components with realistic space around them. For example, a table 120 cm (4 feet) in diameter has room around the perimeter for six chairs (preferably five); chairs need at least 70 cm (2.5 feet) of depth (more if you need to move around the back), requiring a total space of at least 2.6 m (8.5 feet) around for the whole arrangement. Consider the views from various positions in the room; seating, for example, should face an attractive feature. Routes through the room are a consideration, although spaces in which to walk can be quite narrow. Think about the fall of sunlight and the best spot for a lounger. Do not forget storage requirements: do you want a music system, a place for china and glasses or a small concealed fridge for cool drinks and ice?

The heart of the home

The ultimate conservatory for people rather than plants must be a house in which you can live, cook, entertain and work beneath glass. It is an exciting living concept,

Above: A conservatory, rather than being the heart of the home, may contain the living area itself. This contemporary space includes small bedrooms and a bathroom off the large, airy living space.

Left: Conservatory dining areas are practical and pleasantly relaxing, with their views to the outdoor world. In this case, appropriately, an organic vegetable garden is seen through the glass.

'Detailed planning of the position of furniture and fittings is the secret to a practical conservatory for everyday living.'

Below: A family room within easy reach of the garden, kitchen and terrace is a place for meals and gossip. The cloth may be removed and the wicker replaced with dining chairs for evening entertaining.

Right: A formal orangery with pairs of doors, fanlights and a glass roof is set into a brick and stone construction. Designed as part of the garden and next to the outside pool, it also houses changing rooms, kitchen and a fitness room.

and several examples of glasshouse homes are illustrated in this book. I suspect there would be many more built if more locations were suitable, and finding the right one does not always coincide with the practical circumstances to commission, or convert, a glass home. There are practical considerations. Solid walls are essential for bathrooms, stores and utility rooms and for bedrooms (unless there is only one), which also require solid roofs, or suitable black-out blinds. The kitchen will either need to be against a solid wall, perhaps in a recess, or be free-standing, possibly in the centre of the glass living area. This will itself need to be reasonably large, perhaps two-storey, as in the example illustrated on page 30. A fireplace with a solid brick or masonry chimney against one wall for a blazing open fire or, more contemporary in style, a steel cylindrical wood or coal burning stove inside the room, provide both focus and cosiness during the winter.

Suitable locations in cities might occur during urban regeneration, when an old warehouse or industrial space becomes available for housing, possibly on a roof top. Building a conservatory as a home in such a location is a dramatic and inspiring alternative to the loft. The opposite, non-urban, design approach is an orangery set in a formal garden and built single-storey, with bedrooms, bathrooms and so forth constructed at the sides and back – unless the site is steep and the ancillary rooms can be set beneath. This creates the perfect home for a serious gardener and is quite practical. A screen of trees or shrubs, or walls, around the perimeter of the site lends privacy, while cars can be parked out of view behind walls.

An attractive and versatile design idea is to construct (or adopt an existing) substantial brick wall as the centre of the home and to build a large conservatory living area on one side, with solid-construction, additional rooms on the other. The conservatory would open out onto a terrace or grass, while on the other side of the wall would be the house entrance and a yard or garage. Neither side would be visible from the other. Of course,

a conservatory as a home would not be practical without the security or insulation of good double-glazing with automatic blinds for shade or privacy.

Family room conservatories

The reason the majority of conservatories are built is the creation of a family room. A conservatory is an ideal place to be with children: if they are young, it does not matter if they splash paints or spill food; and when older, they can do their homework close to the family. It is a good informal spot for coffee with friends and neighbours, for planning the day, enjoying a leisurely Sunday breakfast and basking in the sun. The environment is perfect. The informal floors and furniture, free from the highly polished surfaces used in most rooms, are perfect for pets: no harm will be done by muddy paws. The glass roof and sides provide plenty of light for reading, writing, sewing, household repairs or games, making the conservatory a natural centre for the practicalities of spare time. With this in mind, plan a room big enough to take at least four chairs – perhaps some comfortable wicker furniture or a sofa upholstered in a practical weave, an armchair or two, a lounger and footstool in a comfortable sunny corner. Design enough space for plants in pots and tubs, and make sure that window sills are wide enough to grow bulbs or herbs. You will need somewhere for a music system and side tables for all the paraphernalia of every-

Above: Older city houses often have small or inconveniently sited kitchens. The solution can be to relocate a kitchen in a conservatory, so that it becomes big enough to use as a family room.

> *'The family room conservatory, with its informal style and practical surfaces, is the ideal place to relax with children and pets, friends and neighbours.'*

day living. I am not a great fan of televisions in conservatories, but if you do have one, position it with the screen facing inwards towards the house, or fit side blinds to the windows and doors to avoid reflections.

Choose warm colours for the paintwork and walls, and for cushions and covers – shades that co-ordinate comfortably with the floor, blinds and furniture. The mix of lighting should include a practical lamp over the main table and effective lamps next to sofas or armchairs for reading or working. Family rooms are used every day and insects may be a problem, especially with children. If it is an occasional problem, fly papers or electrocutors are efficient, but not to everybody's taste; chemical strips and sprays are not very effective in the open environment of a conservatory. If insects are likely to be a serious problem, the conservatory should be built with fly-screens over doors, openable windows and fanlights or roof ventilators. Should insects enter from another part of the house or through an open door, they will be drawn by light to the top of the building; hinged ventilators high in the roof allow them to escape.

A family conservatory can be transformed in the evening into a wonderful, stylish dining room for eating and entertaining – under the stars and surrounded by scented plants, but protected by the warmth and shelter of glass. The table can be set with tiny coloured oil lamps, nightlights or candle hurricane lamps. Alternatively, a hanging chandelier that can be reduced to a candle glow with a dimmer switch will create a gentle, reflected image of the meal in the glass roof. Mirrors on solid walls will reflect the illumination, multiplying the reflections in the glass sides. Depending on the occasion, the table can be covered for the evening with a pretty cloth, informal coloured china and simple glasses, such as decorated Moroccan or painted Bohemian tea glasses with bone or horn-handled cutlery. Ensure that dining chairs have comfortable cushions and that the room is warm; remember that the night temperature in a glass building tends to drop more quickly than that in a solid-walled room. If you

are fortunate and have a fireplace, an open fire in the evening in a glass room has a magical charm. Scented blossom will complete a garden-room meal – generally, scented white flowers are at their most fragrant at night. On a practical note, a conservatory dining room may open directly off the kitchen, or have wide glazed doors that fold back to make communication and serving easy – with the preparation of food in view but not the clutter of pans, pots and washing up.

The kitchen conservatory

The kitchen itself can be built under glass, especially as it will then receive plenty of light and be easy to ventilate: if you need extraction, simply open the roof. If

Above: This kitchen was long and narrow with no seating area and only a small window at the end. The solution was to open up the back of the house into a straightforward, lean-to conservatory, allowing the light to flood in and providing room for a table and chairs.

Overleaf: The combination of pastel colours with the texture of natural stone, wicker, oak and terracotta harmonizes with the crewel work to create a relaxed, soothing interior. This relatively large garden room easily accommodates both sitting and dining space.

the room faces due south, however, the combination of sun and cooking can make it very hot in summer, unless there is shading, excellent ventilation, solar-controlled glass or air conditioning. A kitchen conservatory is an effective, contemporary way of adding a kitchen to a town house; it need not have outward-opening doors, yet it can still link other rooms or passages. Extra space is less likely to be the criteria in the country, but a conservatory kitchen links well with a terrace and is useful if a swimming pool is nearby.

Kitchen worktops are generally 90 cm (3 feet) high and are needed for five functions: food preparation, cooking, serving, washing up and, not least, snacking. Where there is limited space, these areas will be partly combined. The worktops need to be planned logically, to progress from one space to the next and make it possible for two people to work in the kitchen at the same time. Usually these areas are built against a wall – not a problem against a solid wall, but generally impractical against the glazed sides of a conservatory. Unfortunately, even if a conservatory is built on low walls, these are generally only 50-60 cm (about 2 feet) high. Raising them to the necessary level, over a metre (3 feet) in height, rarely looks attractive from outside. The answer is to plan worktops against either existing or purpose-made solid walls, to extend the units out from the solid wall, or to make them completely free-standing within the room. Putting it another way, no work should start until the design of the room and the kitchen layout are both resolved. A kitchen can be incorporated in most instances quite simply if the conservatory is built lengthways along the wall of an existing house, provided there can be at least 5 metres (16 feet) of worktop. Less surface area is needed if preparation, serving or snack area is moved to a free-standing fitting – which can be designed as a handsome piece of furniture.

Above: Although small, this is the dining room of a rambling, eighteenth-century London house. The owners are keen gardeners and the conservatory enables them to enjoy the fine view to the outside.

Plenty of storage is also necessary for an efficient kitchen. Shelves can normally be included, perhaps resting on decorative metal brackets across the windows at eye level, and aligning with the glazing bars of small panes. Practical design considerations are crucial: building the fittings free-standing can be stylish, for example, but requires a large room. This was particularly well resolved in a 6 x 12 m (18 x 36 feet) conservatory I built with architect Valentin Jaquet, who is based in Basle. The interior had sofas at one end, the kitchen towards the other and a dining table in the centre. The dining table was divided from the kitchen area by a purpose-made fitting 2 m (10 feet) in height, consisting of cupboards, glazed at the top, containing china, glasses and cutlery on the dining table side and washing-up facilities and kitchen storage on the other. Preparation and cooking were designed to take place on a square unit behind, at the far end of the conservatory, with a suspended extraction hood going up into the glass roof. I have described this particular example because it provides a simple, logical conservatory solution to the practical concerns of cooking and eating in one space.

Below: This contemporary kitchen is built into a flat-roofed recess, with an airy conservatory opening up in front. The design avoids the fitted kitchen look and combines the two functions of the space with a unified style.

Poolhouses

Where sun and warm weather are unreliable, or wind may prevent the enjoyment of good weather, an indoor swimming-pool is an attractive proposition. A natural development of the garden-room theme, an indoor pool is clean and free from leaves, insects and pests. A pool suitable for swimming lengths – unless it is a tiny exercise pool with a counter-current – needs to be accommodated in a large poolhouse, and it is particularly important to relate its proportions sensitively to those of the original building. As there is no tradition of such domestic buildings, barns and other agricultural styles are often used in country situations, but a glass building provides a lighter, less imposing

alternative. Such designs are usually built in a typical greenhouse or conservatory style, or more grandly, as an eighteenth-century orangery.

Most indoor pools have a straightforward rectangular shape, sometimes with a semi-circle at one end, because this uses space efficiently and allows for an electric pool-cover, which is necessary for safety and to reduce the evaporation and humidity of the room. Typical minimum pool dimensions are 3.5 to 4.5 metres (12 to 15 feet) wide by 8 metres (26 feet) long, and the pool hall will need to be at least two metres (7 feet) longer and wider. Additional structures to house the

pump, filtration equipment, heating and air-conditioning equipment will be required; they need to be built behind a solid wall or even under the ground to avoid the equipment being audible. These extra buildings can turn out to be quite large if they incorporate a room for changing, a shower, a lavatory, kitchen, sauna, solarium and so forth. If built on the reverse side of a poolhouse solid wall, service rooms can often be hidden from view and can possibly be combined with garages and a garden store. Provided that their design is considered as part of the overall scheme, and they are constructed in a simple, workmanlike way with good materials and a well-made roof, they will blend into the setting as attractive, practical outbuildings.

The style of conservatory used for the poolhouse is a matter of taste and will depend partly on the location and style of the surrounding architecture, but there are some special considerations when the building encloses a pool. Plenty of doors opening on to a paved area outside are both functional and decorative, especially if enhanced with delicate fanlights. The view from the pool itself needs to be taken into account, as well as the view from the higher eye level of people sitting or standing. The glazing should be as low or as near to the ground as is practical to avoid obscuring the view out from pool level. When swimming, particularly back stroke, the view of the inside of the roof becomes important, and the logic of its design, the rhythm and pattern of glazing bars and the way components are finished are particularly apparent.

Decorating the poolhouse

A common interior design problem with poolhouses is that the pool itself may present a large and uninteresting void in the middle of the building. Care thus needs to be taken to balance the design and make the area around the pool attractive, with good decorative detailing, bold architectural plants, furniture and a comprehensive colour scheme. Poolhouses are much more appealing to be in if they are finished with

Right: It is often necessary to set the poolhouse some way off from the rest of the house. It will need changing rooms, a toilet, a simple kitchen, storage space and a comfortable place to sit and relax if it is to be a popular and well-used feature. This poolhouse has a furnished conservatory next to it, which links the buildings to the house.

Left: In a temperate climate, a swimming pool must be covered if it is to be reliably usable for more than a few months of the year. Poolhouses are, of necessity, large structures, but using a conservatory achieves a light touch and the inside will have an open, airy feel.

Overleaf: This elevated poolhouse has wonderful views of the surrounding trees. The pool equipment, changing rooms, fitness area, kitchen and study are contained beneath.

Above: When swimming lengths, glimpses of a conservatory structure, with its rhythm of doors and rafters, is satisfying. The clean, uncluttered space shown here has a calm colour scheme, with both the pool interior and floor tiled in the same stone. The end opens fully on to a terrace with a view down to a sunken garden.

attractive, good-quality materials: a sandstone or limestone floor, for example, perhaps using the same material on the inside of the pool to avoid the cheap look of most mosaic linings. Subtly textured stucco on the solid walls, combined with soft-coloured paintwork, enhances the interior design. If roof blinds are used, their colour and woven texture will contribute towards softening the lines of the room, but to be practical they must be electrically operated, in the same way as the pool cover.

It is usual to have several lamps set beneath the surface of the water, alternating along each side. This can

be supplemented with spot lamps, positioned so that they will not cause glare, to wash light over the walls, starlights in the roof to provide background lighting and hanging lamps from the centre of the roof, usually best with a restrained, minimalist design. Lamps can be set at regular intervals around the framing, both inside and out, but all internal lighting must be low-voltage for safety. A the same time, the roof can be wired for (splash-proof) speakers, although the system will need to be powerful to enjoy reasonably loud music.

The individual character of a poolhouse is further enhanced by choosing plants that suit its space. By their

> *'Light, water and foliage in conservatory poolhouses combine both to invigorate and relax. The reflected framework reveals the movement of water in rippling pattern.'*

nature, the buildings are large, perhaps even palatial in scale and the interior design is generally relatively spare, functional and masculine in style. They provide a perfect environment for stately, slow-growing architectural plants: palms, large citrus – perhaps a grapefruit – olive trees or even tree ferns growing in large, heavy and permanently positioned pots. Climbers provide a decorative complement to tall walls and ceilings and can help the large structure to harmonize with the outdoor scene, as well as screening the blank central area inside. Outside the poolhouse, a private area should be made for relaxing and sunbathing close to the pool; if it is some way from the house kitchen, a separate small kitchen or bar is essential. There may also be service buildings to accommodate, perhaps echoing the style of the main building. Good lighting outdoors, as well as in and around the poolhouse, is essential.

Practical details

A typical poolhouse will have floor space two metres (*c.*7 feet) wide around at least two sides, plus an area to sit and relax close by. A high proportion of doors opening on to a paved area outside will ensure maximum use of the poolhouse during good weather. If the change of level between the floor of the poolhouse and the paving outside is kept to a minimum, the resulting flow of air will help to keep the room cool; and the poolhouse surround will be effectively larger with the doors open, with less risk of tripping if somebody, especially a child, runs to the pool.

Plenty of ventilation will be essential to keep the room cool in warm weather, with lots of openable doors and roof ventilators. They are best controlled with a thermostatic system, which also monitors and controls the heating. The alternative – full air conditioning – requires the building to be closed, which reduces the sense of a link with the garden beyond. When air conditioning is used, it is important to stress that it should be unobtrusive. The air, which can be heated up as well as cooled and either dried or humidified, needs to re-

circulate with a small proportion of fresh air added, and flow and return grilles are needed. Where the poolhouse is built against an existing house or another structure, a grille can be placed at high level against the solid side, and positioned at floor level around the perimeter of the external, glazed side.

In cool weather, water heating, coupled with warm-air heating to keep the air temperature a couple of degrees above that of the water, is usual. To minimize condensation, dehumidify the air in the pool hall; in conjunction with low-emissivity double-glazing, this solution is normally effective.

Above: When swimming, the surroundings are viewed from an eye-level close to the ground. To provide an attractive perspective, the glass in doors or windows should extend down as low as possible.

The Working Conservatory

rtists such as painters, jewellers and silver-smiths may work happily at home in a conservatory-studio – indeed, I have known many who do just that – but for the majority of us, work requires some form of office. Taking the office home avoids the noise and inter-ruption of working with other people, and with low phone costs, fax and email it is now feasible. For many, being at home also means having to avoid distractions, which necessitates a separate room. A conservatory can be quiet and calm and far less oppressive than a con-ventional, solid-walled room, particularly if it is small. Grey computer boxes never look attractive, and moni-tors less so the larger they become. Flat screens are considerably neater and their extra cost may be com-pensated for by the space they save and the lower risk of radiation. Laptops are the least obtrusive options, although they will still need some cables. Whatever the screen, reflections can be avoided by facing it back towards a solid wall; and if it is flat, roof shading is essential for it to appear sufficiently bright to see prop-erly. Everyone uses their own form of filing (mine is concertina files), but buy or have built a cupboard to hide it in, along with paper and the inevitable office clut-ter. Use a wireless phone or a mobile, and treat yourself to attractive folders and accessories. Combine these with a comfortable conservatory chair and table and an effi-cient office set-up will assimilate naturally into a garden room. Avoid too many plants in the space, however, as they will need and create too much humidity.

Security

Unless you live in a situation where it is unimportant, there are two approaches to maintaining security in a garden-room office. One is to make the opening between the conservatory and the house secure and keep nothing of great value in the conservatory. The other is to make the room secure and, if an alarm system is fitted, part of the secure 'envelope' – essential if the conservatory is also used as a living room and if it opens directly onto another room. I have the notion that a burglar might try the conservatory first in the belief that it is the easiest way into the house, and then be thoroughly repelled when he finds he is wrong.

First, make sure that a timber conservatory is constructed of hardwood and that it has security bolts on openable windows. If the doors are designed to open outwards, employ hinge bolts (which make it impossible to lift out a door by simply driving the pins from the hinges) and use secure door locks. Tall or double doors are easier to operate if they have a lever fitting which simultaneously locks them top and bottom, and better still in the middle as well. Espagnolette bolts fit the bill; traditional, surface-mounted ones are attractive, but nowhere near as secure as those fitted into the thickness of the door. Next, make sure that the glass is toughened and, for the highest

Above: Working at home usually turns out to be more of a chore than you imagined when packing your office case. However, in the environment of a conservatory, with a comfortable chair and an attractive view, it will be far more rewarding.

Right: The tiny, practical conservatory I built for myself on a house in Kensington uses the shady side for bookcases.

degree of security, use a combination of toughened and laminated double-glazing. Last, alarm the room and make sure the fittings will be visible from outside. Movement detectors, 'tremblers', are good fitted around the framework because they operate the alarm and drive off the intruder before he (or she) has gained entry; and they also permit use of the room with the alarm still on. Make sure that roof ventilators are alarmed. If greater security is required, fit a vertical roller shutter between the conservatory and house, and use a thick, multi-layer, laminated form of glass.

Living with plants
Although in most instances the first purpose of the conservatory is as a room for people – and a modern, double-glazed construction would not be cost-effective otherwise – I always feel at least a moment's disappointment when visiting a conservatory that houses no plants. Conservatory style is steeped in horticulture, and with the light, warmth and protection that a glasshouse provides, it seems wrong not to have at least an orange tree flowering in a tub or a jasmine climbing up a wall. Many people regard conservatory gardening as difficult and specialized, especially once they have tried to maintain indoor plants. Yet there is a difference, because indoor plants are inevitably grown in very poor light, often coming just from one side, on a draughty window-sill or dry corner where watering and maintenance are awkward. By contrast, in a conservatory there should be a convenient water supply and it does not matter if the floor or walls receive an occasional splash. Conservatory plants are usually bigger and are grown in

'Contemporary greenhouse-style conservatories celebrate the horticultural roots of garden rooms. They offer protection for tender, exotic plants, as well as those that thrive outdoors.'

larger containers, needing less precise watering at greater intervals. You do not need to be a trained expert in order to succeed in a conservatory. First of all, an understanding of the basic culture requirements of the plants you wish to grow, and of whether your conservatory can offer them, is needed. Then you must ensure careful root-watering and develop a habit of looking at plants and noticing the condition of their foliage, when new buds are appearing and if they have attracted greenfly or stopped growing for some reason. Calculate where in the room they do best, and take prompt action if you notice a problem.

The type of plants grown will depend on the other uses of the room and its decoration. In a kitchen conservatory, the emphasis is most likely to be culinary – indoor herbs such as chervil, coriander, basil and thyme, grown in a bright spot. A lemon or orange tree (more for the idea than for steady cropping of fruit),

Below: In a carefully designed and planted walled garden, a standard greenhouse would be out of place. Here I raised up the walls in the corner to accommodate the radiating rafters for a conservatory-style greenhouse, quarter-round in plan. The roof has scallop-cut overlapping panes.

and lemon-scented geraniums, ginger or cardamom will perfume the air. Resist the temptation to grow a grapevine in the kitchen, however, as it is not practical. One or a pair of huge, magnificent plants (such as the pair of alocassias illustrated on page 6) provide a specific garden-room focus in a smartly decorated space where the primary purpose is definitely not horticulture. Suitable plants are architectural – that is, generally evergreen, dependent on their foliage rather than blossom for interest – and are easy to manage with low humidity. Many palms fit these criteria. Small-leafed *Ficus benjamina* will grow almost anywhere to a large size, while *Musa*, the banana family, produces lush, giant-leafed herbs which, in some cases and with plenty of light, can fruit in an ordinary conservatory. Large cacti can be included in this category of sculptural plants, but their problem, of course, is not lack of humidity but too much of it.

Just as a sculpture needs a good plinth, these stylish plants must have a beautiful, complementary pot or tub: a metre (3 feet) high, hand-thrown terracotta pot; a venerable marble urn (with suitable drainage); or a contemporary or traditional lead tub. The plant and container together become an important element of the interior decoration, and thought will have to be given to its logical location – in terms both of the furniture layout and the plant's needs.

While one or two fine, large plants may provide an interior focus, they will not satisfy a real passion for Victorian-style indoor gardening. A Victorian conservatory was a superior greenhouse, built as an envelope over a hot and humid micro-world of lush plants, the only access to the garden being doors wide enough for a gardener with a barrow. Inside, the space was densely filled, typically with a central bed of well-rooted trees and tall shrubs and staging around the perimeter with serried ranks of pot plants. Space beneath became a mass of ferns amongst the heating pipes, while that above contained assorted hanging baskets, climbers and overhanging fronds. In a suitable corner might be

placed a marble-topped, cast-iron table and chairs to take tea and gossip. As a venue for intrigue or romance, the conservatory became a nineteenth-century novelists' cliché. In modern garden rooms it is not impractical to nurture and build a good, scaled-down collection of plants, while using the room domestically and socially much more than its predecessor. For success, the two areas must be reasonably defined, with the preferred area for plants having priority. The watering of plants, the dampness of their soil and pots and the humidity around their foliage can to some extent be contained and concentrated for the benefit of adjacent plants by keeping them close together. They can be arranged along a single wall, across one end or even as a cluster in the centre of the conservatory. As long as there are no fabrics or rugs in these areas, and furniture is kept a little apart, plants can be easily and freely watered. If there is underfloor heating in a trench, perhaps one that doubles as a drain, then any water which gets in will evaporate and increase the humidity of the garden room. Cultivated in this way, the majority of the plants

Above: An attractive allotment greenhouse, constructed from second-hand doors and windows and an old corrugated roof, produces great quantities of fruit and vegetables.

Right: The conservatory on my London home, viewed from outside, shows the store of old terracotta pots for indoor and terrace gardening.

described in Chapter 6 can be easily and successfully grown. Staging benches are useful; they look good in their own right and enable plants to be packed close together, yet still make the most of the available light. And if they have a gravel tray, small or young plants can be conveniently cultivated and easily watered. Unless you decide to devote the space entirely to plants, propagation, apart from a few seeds, is best relegated to a separate, utilitarian greenhouse. Bulbs past their best, other flowering plants that are less interesting without blossom – such as most orchids – or even sickly plants in need of hospitalization can be relegated there. How-

Left: As they are gradually disappearing, it is well worth buying old, hand-thrown flowerpots whenever you see them for sale. They are easy to clean in a dishwasher, and they should be stored stacked sideways to minimize cracking.

'In garden rooms designed primarily for people, the serious business of gardening is best despatched to the garden shed outside. A space dedicated to plants, however, allows the conservatory gardener scope for imaginative experiment.'

ever, a few annual seeds, such as ipomoea or thunbergia, will not be out of place sprouting on a window-sill. Space for potting is required – perhaps the main table with a sheet of stiff plastic over it – as is a cupboard for storing compost and sundries, although it is generally better to use a shed outside with a solid, working-height bench for this purpose. A stock of flowerpots is best stacked neatly and attractively in the garden (assuming they are clay and not plastic).

Training plants against walls is not only a good use of available space, but is also an attractive and appropriate way of treating plain areas of solid wall in the garden room. It needs to be done neatly, with everything steel-galvanized or painted. Use wedge-shaped, traditional vine eyes for straining wires, positioning them with a tape measure and level and fitting the wires in a workmanlike way. Otherwise, use trellis, perhaps of painted timber or wirework panels, as it needs to be more refined than the ready-made garden type. To encourage climbers to cover the trellis evenly, shoots should be pinched out before they are too high to encourage fresh growth at the bottom. Growing climbers in the roof is best done with wires set well below the glass, at about 30 cm (12 in). This keeps the glazing clean and allows space for roof blinds. However, vigorous climbers need regular pinching out to keep them under control.

Right: The greenhouse conservatory at the previous country home of antique dealer Christopher Gibbs has a traditional terracotta floor, black Homberg grapevine and a collection of attractive conservatory antiques.

3

Construction and Design

Modern conservatories can be influenced by a wide range of architectural styles, from the traditional orangery and glasshouse to the most innovative poolhouse or garden room. The term conservatory embraces a wide variety of structures: they may be connected to houses or freestanding; palatial or unassuming, greenhouse-like buildings that reflect their horticultural origins. Glass remains the dominant ingredient, although new, more sophisticated glazing, heating and ventilation have transformed its use, and designs of the past can be re-intrepreted for people as well as plants. As most garden rooms are adjuncts to existing buildings, it is important to choose materials and architecture that complement the house and make the most of available space.

Selecting the Style

The distinctive character of a conservatory depends upon its architectural framework and the materials from which it is devised. Traditional designs draw upon two themes – the classical orangery and the later, more elaborate, cast-iron structure that celebrates the versatility of metalwork. Each can provide a style for a contemporary construction, but, in either case, a conservatory needs to work with the interior design and suit the scale of the existing building in order to bring a balanced addition to the site.

The earliest orangeries showed conscious classical resonances in their architecture. They were often substantial stone buildings, initially with solid roofs, and decorated with balustrades, columns or pilasters and cornices. Tall and broad sash windows, which might be raised high enough for an entrance, filled the spaces between round columns. The proportions followed strict classical precepts. The widespread availability of expensive cast iron in the nineteenth century led to an explosion of decoration. Catalogues advertised castings not only for windows and doors, but also for ornamental details: brackets, panels, crestings, finials, grilles for heating and braces added to roof trusses. In addition, conservatories became quicker to design and construct, as a limited number of castings were ingeniously combined and repeated. Clever joints and metal wedges held the ironwork together, and fanlights, roof lanterns, projected gables and elaborate moulding were often included in the intricate structures. Cast iron, prone to rusting and condensation, is little used today, but the exuberant decoration associated with it has inspired many modern designers.

Decorative details

When looking at the conventions of conservatory design, it is important to consider what will work in a particular environment. Even if it is not directly linked to the house, a conservatory should reflect existing elements of the architecture that it serves. Many features can often be incorporated in a carefully related, reduced scale.

Left: An essentially symmetrical design has the conservatory shifting the emphasis from the sides to the centre of the Cotswold stone house and its garden. The umber paintwork has been selected to harmonize with the existing local stonework.

Right: Bold timber columns and a classical framework reminiscent of an eighteenth-century orangery have been used to create a distinctive style for this modern conservatory.

Unusually, the entire structure of a conservatory is visible, and the construction itself comprises the decoration, and vice versa, creating a clearly defined architectural style. From mullion to moulded cornice, patterned glazing bars to pilasters, decoration and structure are integrated into the design. Gutters may be moulded to form cornices – but also collect and discharge rainwater – or held on cast brackets to highlight the junctions and divisions of the framework behind. Similarly, an internal cornice demarcates walls and roof and brings architectural interest, yet it can also conceal roller blinds and lamp fittings. Conservatory roofs, in fact, offer a great opportunity for architectural display – inside with mouldings and brackets, and outside with finials, cresting and cornices. Some may echo the elaborate gables and bargeboards of the larger house to which they are attached. Whether inside or outside, it is important that all conservatory details are in proportion and of suitable materials, and that they are in keeping with the overall design.

Harmonizing with existing buildings

There is often little choice about the location of a conservatory, especially on a city site with limited space. Design flexibility is important here: a conservatory built on top of a brick extension, for example, can borrow

Above: Gables used here as a design feature not only emphasize the geometry of the roof, but also that of the two entrances – one at the end and the other facing down across a lawn. In this instance, the gables are in keeping with the profiles of the house roof.

Left: Older city houses are generally much less attractive at the back than at the front, but this can be remedied with a smartly designed conservatory. This example has diamond-pane fanlights, which lend a garden-room trellis style.

Architectural Details

Decorative details of a conservatory should be chosen to enhance the structural framework. They should complement one another in style and proportion, emphasizing and refining the architectural theme.

Above: A bold, elaborately turned urn finial is suitable for a building in a classical design.

Above right: Turned timber or metal finials not only decorate the apex of a roof, but also provide a practical finish to the posts around which timber roofs are constructed.

Left: A cast-metal Doric capital adorns a classical building. A zinc lantern is fixed beneath against the pilaster.

Right: Victorian-style *par excellence* is apparent here, with reproduction carving, mouldings, leaded lights with coloured and cut glass – and a cast-metal finial.

Left: An antique ram's-head capital is used to decorate a functional supporting column. To succeed, such decorative details should be used logically and assimilated into the construction of the building.

Right: Hi-tech is combined with period detail: the Gothic gingerbread used to complement the original features of the adjoining historic house belies high-performance double-glazing and automatic ventilation control.

and develop features to create a specific, appropriate building for the site. Suburban or country settings may offer a greater but more complex range of possibilities. For the greatest freedom of design, the simplest location is best – an open setting, or against a single wall.

Orientating the conservatory correctly often requires imagination and ingenuity, as each setting is different. Architecture that emphasizes symmetry, such as a Georgian house, may be best with a conservatory set slightly apart, with a link to the main building, so that it does not compromise the design. If symmetry is to be deliberately broken, it is often best to create a detached appearance for the new building – for example, a hipped roof with its back slope running down to the house. The building thus appears to be constructed against, rather than growing organically out of, the house.

The style of an existing building can be echoed in a variety of ways. A conservatory base may use the materials and construction of the existing building, for example, and pilasters with a moulded cornice reflect the features of original woodwork. Fanlights introduce a decorative frieze, height and a delicate touch to a solid, orangery-like structure. An asymmetrical, vernacular-style house may invite a lantern roof or decorative gables, ornamental brackets, fanlights, coloured glass or ridge decoration. It is well worth investigating the plans of an old building for any record of an earlier conservatory that could be reinstated or used as inspiration – and if the building is historically listed, consent will be much easier to obtain.

Glazing bars are the distinctive feature of a traditional conservatory, dividing up the glazed area to create a pattern and rhythm to the design. They lend either a horizontal or vertical emphasis and modify the scale of the doors, windows, fanlights and gables. The possibilities include small domestic glazing panes with upright proportions and plain vertical bars, perhaps with a single horizontal line, reminiscent of the great earlier glasshouses at Chatsworth and Kew Gardens.

Adding the familiar semicircles, as shown above, or the gothic glazing patterns illustrated overleaf contributes a distinctive rhythm and interest. This can be used to excess, however, and is generally best restricted to small areas, such as fanlights and gables. Such attractive windows add a liberating feeling of height and decoration to a conservatory, especially if small panes are also used elsewhere, perhaps to reflect the window style of the house itself. Harmonizing the proportions of window panes and bars is one of the most effective ways to make visual connections between the existing building and a new conservatory.

Above: A rhythm of half- and quarter-circles adds vibrancy and unifies the exterior sides and internal doors of this city conservatory.

Left: A combination of horizontal, vertical and diagonal thin glazing bars in the doors, fanlights and roof of the conservatory are echoed in the design of its furniture.

Overleaf: Pictured here is the main façade of an orangery I designed, with carefully set out details and each brick and stone precisely located. Such care plays an important part in the overall success of the decorative design.

Doors and Windows

Well-proportioned doors and windows are an important element of good conservatory construction. The balance and scale of panes and bars, whether in small fanlights or large double doors, bring a harmony to the design.

Above: The charm of this decoration of Gothic ogee tracery is due in part to the geometrical logic of the design, but also to the delicate glazing bars. These designs are best executed with single-glazing, allowing bars as slim as 15 mm.

Left: Situated at the top of the glazing, the curved work – a variation on Gothic decoration – leaves a relatively clear area in the body of the door or window.

Above: Fanlights add height to a structure and create a horizontal line which, if decorated, makes a 'frieze' above the doors and beneath the roof.

Left: A single-glazed conservatory shows a much simplified version of Gothic decoration that lends graceful shape and height to the doors.

'For well over a century – from the magnificent Crystal Palace housing London's Great Exhibition of 1851 to I.M. Pei's inspirational pyramid at the Louvre in Paris in 1989 – metal and glass structures have been objects of delight.'

Above: Hard-to-break, highly insulating double-glazing has made glass buildings such as this secure and comfortable, and usable all year round.

Right: The decorative entrance gable of a 1900s conservatory shows a simple building with single, 3 mm glazing into decorative softwood framing. This allows for great decorative versatility, but depends on cheap heating and continuous maintenance.

Building with glass

Glass is the key, defining ingredient in conservatory construction and design. The way in which it shapes walls and ceilings and the transparent screen it creates distinguishing inside from outside worlds determine architectural impact, comfort and practicality. The technology of glass is constantly evolving, and contemporary conservatory design can take advantage of improved insulation, reduced condensation and opportunities to use glass in many new ways.

The combination in the nineteenth century of cheaper glass and adaptable cast iron radically changed the relative proportions of materials in a building. Glass became the dominant element in delicate, imaginative structures, although only single-glazing was possible, with small panes and closely spaced glazing bars. Curved roofs, such as that of Bicton Hall in Devon, were achieved by overlapping a series of flat glass panes. The imperfections of old glass add to its character and charm, so glass from, say, old greenhouses, provides the closest match for renovating an existing conservatory. The condensation problems of single-glazing may be reduced if part of the structure, for example the roof, is double-glazed with toughened glass.

Following the development of high-quality float glass in the 1960s, sealed-unit double-glazing (see page 75) transformed insulation techniques. Together with low-emissivity glass, this opened up further possibilities for modifying glass used in large-scale constructions. Security glass, previously made with a fine-wire mesh embedded in the glass but now largely replaced by clear, laminated or tempered glass, also enables larger panes to be used safely. It has enabled the production of large structural glass panes which can be assembled with a lightweight framework or even frameless constructions of striking pyramidal or cuboid minimalism. Such contemporary design depends on air conditioning and generally lacks windows and external doors. These structures work particularly well in modern urban settings, for example a roof terrace or paved area.

Clear security glass is a sandwich construction of invisible plastic with glass on each side, while laminated glass varies in thickness from approximately 5 mm to 20 mm (1.25 to 5 in). The latter is heavy and expensive, but provides the ultimate in security, being rated to NATO standards for bullet resistance (very useful if assassination is a possibility). The more usual, thinner laminated glass is still difficult to break, but has little resistance to cracking. Tempered glass, on the other hand, is made by heating, and then rapidly cooling, float glass to create tensions within it, making it stronger and more flexible. A side-effect of this process is to make the surface slightly uneven, reminiscent of the wobbles in antique glass, a possible advantage for a traditional conservatory style. Sealed units with an outer leaf of tempered glass for strength and an inner layer of laminate glass for security are also available.

Single-glazing continues to be used today because, although it is far less insulating, it is light, can work in small pieces and requires a frame rebate of only 6 mm in depth. This allows glazing bars as slim as 15 mm, compared with the European Standard of 35 mm-wide bars for double-glazing with sealed units. Single-glazing is easily installed with traditional linseed oil putty. Plastic glazing (PVC, acrylic, or, best, polycarbonate polymers) is maunfactured specially for roofs with multiple layers divided into separate channels, which makes them strong, light and difficult to break, with excellent insulation. However, most plastic glazing is not transparent, and becomes progressively more opaque as the exterior surface is scratched over time by minute fine particles of atmosphere grit. It also expands and contracts with temperature changes far more than glass does, creaking within its framework as it warms or cools. Plastic is easy to bend for barrel-shaped or domed roofs, but only as single-glazing. Curved, sealed units of glass can be made, but usually the skill and labour involved make the cost prohibitive.

Above: Leaded lights offer great versatility and intricacy of design, but are single-glazed and so best suited for use in small areas, such as these fanlights. Self-adhesive lead strips are sometimes applied to double-glazing in imitation of real leaded lights, which are made by soldering lead strips together around pieces of shaped glass.

Materials and Structure

The choice of materials in any room strongly influences its feel and style. In a conservatory, the textures and surfaces of materials normally associated with the outdoors – brick, stone, timber, terracotta and metal – influence the play of light and the effect of colour. Smooth and shiny surfaces are very reflective, with an almost overwhelming visual echo if large expanses of glass and water are involved. Matt surfaces will absorb more light and appear warmer, perhaps making the space usable in winter months. All materials possess their own characteristics, potential and limitations, although these can be partially modified by finishes such as varnish or paint. Certain elements may dominate a room, but none exist in isolation, and the impact of each depends on its relation with others. All conservatory materials must be durable and resistant to heat or damp, but they exist in enough variety to allow the creation of imaginative designs.

Brick and stone

These traditional building materials provided the fabric of early orangeries, typified by solid, substantial masonry frameworks divided by large pairs of French doors. The front of an orangery would be symmetrical, with odd numbers – usually three, five or seven – of door sets. This construction lent a solidity and permanence to a rather grand style of building, not suited to every location but more enduring than many of the iron and glass constructions that succeeded it. The architectural emphasis on high sides and relatively inconspicuous inset roofs can provide a good contemporary solution when overall height is limited or the view from a first-floor window may otherwise be obscured. To be successful, a glass building constructed with brick or stone needs well-considered details and proportions. The physical properties of masonry – strong in compression, weak in tension, and so deriving strength from the weight of material – should also be considered. Orangeries are usually designed to sit solidly on a plinth or surrounding steps, so the floor level may need to be higher than the surrounding garden. The attraction of good, well-constructed masonry derives in part from the use of carefully sized and arranged brickwork or stonework, or a mix of both (see pages 62-3). The French doors in orangery-style construction traditionally had the glazing extended down close to the floor, rather than hip height, as is the case with the majority of timber-framed conservatories.

Indoors, the texture and colour of brick, stone, marble and slate retain an earthiness, with a natural palette of soft greys, umber and ochre. Interiors of brick or stone were mostly smoothly finished with plaster, but for an architectural effect, an interior can be painted and, if of soft, old materials, sealed to prevent dusting.

Right: Combining a timber and glass framework on two sides with brick construction on the other creates a sense of openness on the side facing the gardens and a secure, solid feel on the boundary side. The stone floor and fireplace, colour of the woodwork and the shades used in the brickwork were picked to complement one another.

Below: A brick-framed, orangery-style building has an unusual curved front, which masks a flat roof with a large, inset glazed lantern.

Floors

Unless the conservatory floor runs through from an adjoining room, its style and material will probably change at the threshold, emphasizing entry to a different kind of space. It will need to be practical – fitted carpets will fade and quickly mark, and polished, plain finishes easily become scratched and stained.

Before settling on the material, consider the floor in relation to the outside as well as to the adjacent rooms. Will there be a step down to the terrace and garden, and should the materials indoors and out be similar? The allusions made by garden rooms to the world outside can be emphasized by selecting natural, textured materials for the floor: limestone, slate, brick and

Above: Conservatory floors need to be durable and rather permanent features, and they justify an expense of care and individuality in their design.

'The floor of the conservatory is an important visual link between the interior life of the house and the natural world outside, and its material should provide flow between the two.'

terracotta, sandstone or ceramic tiles. For example, I have used old, worn sandstone outside on a terrace, changing to new, smooth sandstone within the conservatory. If the doors are folded back in summer, the relationship between inside and out will be especially apparent. Use practical materials that will not be affected by sunlight or water, and are easy to maintain, and resist even attractive materials if they will not wear well.

Most natural flooring materials come in a variety of sizes from a few centimetres square up to a metre in length. Successful use will depend in part on the shape, size and pattern that is adopted. Stone can be bought as squares or rectangles (1–3 cm/ 0.4–1.2 in thick); lay it randomly or in a grid pattern – coursed like rows of bricks or diamond fashion, with small insets at the corners. Stone is usually ordered 'honed', with a smooth but matt finish. Occasionally it is purchased with edges ground to give a worn effect, or 'flamed' – a process of heating the surface until it blisters away, leaving an attractive texture. This is often used around pools for a non-slip edge. Joints between tiles are filled with grout, manufactured in cream, beige, grey and black. A shade usually matches the flooring tiles, but a strong pattern can be emphasized with a contrasting colour.

The various types of stone discussed below are those most commonly used for conservatory floors.
Limestone. The most popular material for floors, limestone ranges in colour and texture from smooth, near-white forms to fossil-flecked sienna, rust-streaked burgundy, spotted Portuguese stone and warm-textured Cotswold flags. It also varies in hardness: select a soft, crumbly looking stone for an outdoor or country effect, and a smooth, hard one for an urban style. Note that most limestone is not frost-proof.
Terracotta. Red shades are most commonly available, but often difficult to use in colour schemes. Paler cream, buff or pink versions are best, especially if they are handmade, with beautiful variations in colour and texture made by mixing clays and firing the tiles in

Above: Here the floor incorporates traditional encaustic tiles, arranged to make a pattern to complement the Gothic, ecclesiastical style of the building.

Left: Cast-iron grilles not only cover underfloor heating, but can also be treated as the border around the perimeter of the conservatory floor.

'Stone is a material that seems to absorb all its past history, giving an authentic, timeless feel to a conservatory floor.'

traditional wood ovens. Such tiles are generally small, usually under 30 cm long, and they are not frost-proof.

Sandstone. Tough and available in large sizes, sandstone is suitable for big conservatories. It is generally grey or warm browny-buff, and is occasionally streaked, sometimes in violent patterns. It is frost-proof and extremely hard-wearing.

Marble. Of the same composition as limestone, marble is a smooth and sometimes slightly translucent stone. It is the grandest flooring material, available in an extraordinarily wide range of textures and colours, including black and white. Its usual commercial high polish can easily be removed with acid treatment after laying if required. Some forms, such as travertine, have striations and a pitted surface, which when filled and sealed create an attractive, antique appearance.

Other flooring materials include inexpensive cement-based tiles, which are best textured, but not in imitation of natural stone, as this effect gradually wears away. Resin-bonded stone is smart and sparkling, and is available in brilliant colours for a contemporary look. Wood is not good with water, and will shrink in sunlight to develop gaps, but tough, unvarnished hardwoods, such as oak laid in broad boards, make

Above: An old, gently decayed look is created in this new conservatory with antique marble flooring, combined with lime-plastered walls and cast-iron covered underfloor heating.

Left: Conservatory floors are best in mellow materials which allow traffic to flow in and out to the garden. Unlike carpet, they cannot easily be changed and so classic materials, unaffected by the vagaries of fashion but complementing the room's other textures and colours, are most successful. In this instance, terracotta has been combined with oak framing and skirting boards.

Floor Finishes

Simple, natural-looking materials, such as brick, limestone, slate and sandstone, are traditional and will link the style of the conservatory to the outdoors. They can be used either singly or in combination to make borders and patterns around a floor.

Left: English terracotta contains natural variations in colour, both within and between individual tiles. Its beautiful soft-red hues bring a sense of sun and warmth to a shady conservatory and can soften more formal materials, such as marble, sandstone or slate.

Right: Moroccan glazed terracotta tiles can easily be cut and laid in arrangements, as in this example, in harlequin pattern.

Left: Antique terracotta has a beautiful, crumbly texture. When buying second-hand material, check each tile individually and make sure there is enough for the job – more may not be available later.

Right: Pale buff Cotswold stone laid in a simple grid and waxed-finished. This is applied over a clear seal which soaks into the stone and resists oil, water and grease stains.

Left: Brick paviors have a strongly outdoor style and an uneven texture. Avoid brick red and use paler Cambridge paviors assembled into an interesting pattern.

Right: Antique marble is a matt-textured Italian stone which introduces a feeling of permanence to a garden room. Its creamy buff colour suits a pale look.

handsome, textured floors. For a really rustic look, use secondhand bricks – or purpose-made paviors, which are harder and thinner – laid in herringbone or brick coursing. Most floors can be treated with a transparent, nearly invisible sealer, which effectively repels grease and water marks. This must be applied immediately after the laying of the floor, before the room is used.

Timber construction

Wood is well suited to the construction of domestic conservatories. It is easily worked and shaped, and therefore has immense flexibility of use as a building material. The texture, grain and minor imperfections that are found in timber only add to its overall character. It has good insulation properties and works well with double-glazing to make warm, condensation-free rooms. A good complement to stone or brick, timber is a useful material for blending old and new styles. It can be cut easily to make decorative brackets, turned finials and fretwork and mouldings to match existing woodwork.

Wood is a natural material that should be used only as a renewable resource. Softwoods, such as pine and cedar, grow in sub-arctic regions, and most countries have replanting programmes (although Russia is a major exception). Softwoods are generally strong and, apart from cedar, need to be impregnated with preservatives to make them durable. They are smooth, mark easily (particularly cedar) and require varnish or paint as a protective layer. Hardwood for conservatories, with a few exceptions, usually means tropical, mahogany-like timber. It is more expensive than softwood, but can be very durable, strong, hard and easily paintable without preservative (in fact, most hardwoods cannot be impregnated with preservative). The best hardwoods can be beautifully finished and they warp or twist very little. They are the ideal choice for good-quality woodwork, but do ask about the timber's origins and whether there are effective re-planting schemes in place at source. Supplies certified by Forests Forever (Clareville House, 26/27 Oxendon Street, London SW1Y 4EL tel: 020 7839 1891) or by

Above: Timber has a reassuring, soft appearance and is pleasant to walk on, but it will shrink and show cracks when exposed to sunlight. When using timber, ensure the location is shaded or lay the floor in a rustic style with unpolished boards so that imperfections are not an issue.

Timber for Conservatories

Timber has a role in both the construction and decoration of conservatories. It is an attractive and versatile material, and it responds well to turning, carving, moulding and the individual requirements of bespoke work. When used outdoors, it needs routine maintenance.

Far left: Wooden brackets with shaped ends are employed to decorate the underside of a box gutter around a glass roof.

Left: Instead of plaster or render, the inside walls can be finished with match-boarding for a warm, woody style. Here wide boards have joints masked with small, half-round beads to complement the door.

Far left: This conservatory celebrates, rather than hides, its wooden construction. It is jettied like a traditional timber-framed house.

Left: Timber can be extended outside to make a deck, although the exterior may need more robust finishing.

> *'Last century's advances in glass technology were astonishing, creating a very versatile building material.'*

the Forest Stewardship Council (FSC UK, Unit D, Station Building, Llanidloes, Powys, Wales SY18 6EB tel: 01686 413 916) are reliable.

The choice and quality of timber is also controlled, especially for durability, by European building regulations and some US codes. If the natural texture and colour of unpainted wood are preferred, temperate hardwoods are usually the best choice: oak and ash are especially attractive, but they will need to be sealed and resealed regularly on the exterior to maintain the finish and prevent natural silvering. Provided that the wood was well seasoned to begin with and has been carefully constructed and finished, painted timber will last for hundreds of years.

Types of glass

Contemporary conservatory design would be impractical without the developments in glass technology that have been made during the last thirty years. These include sealed-for-life double-glazing that reliably works; security glass that is difficult to break and, if it does, is not dangerous (see page 65); barely visible coatings that greatly improve the insulating capacity of double-glazing; and treatments that control the penetration of ultraviolet light or heat gain in sunlight. Developed for commercial buildings, these technologies are now practical at a domestic scale. A conservatory may now be used all the year round in a wide range of climates with realistic heating costs and minimal condensation.

The styles and modifications of glass buildings have followed the steady improvements in glass technology. Traditional methods of production included blowing molten glass into a cylinder, which was then cut and flattened, or spinning molten discs (crown glass) to about a metre in diameter, and then cutting them into individual panes when cool. Industrial production of rolled glass in the 1840s made construction of large-scale glasshouses feasible. Float glass, invented in the 1960s, involved the floating of a continuous ribbon of

cooling glass across a large pool of molten tin. It created a virtually blemish-free product of consistent thickness.

Modern sealed-unit double-glazing has overcome many of the condensation and insulation problems that characterized early glasshouses. The space inside a sealed unit, between the two pieces of glass, is filled with dehumidified air; if certain inert gases, such as argon or more expensive xenon, are used instead, the

Left: The window looks out to a dark wall, so the addition of a lantern roof made this large bathroom considerably brighter, without loss of privacy. It also allows the romance of bathing with a view of the stars.

Opposite: Boldly coloured leaded lights are used as the central feature in a conservatory built as a restaurant. The coloured panels are set inside the roof beneath the double-glazing.

Below: An iron and glass roof is added to cover an internal courtyard at Mezquita in Cordoba. It has an interesting, satisfyingly geometrical plan, and is assembled with thousands of sparkling, overlapping panes.

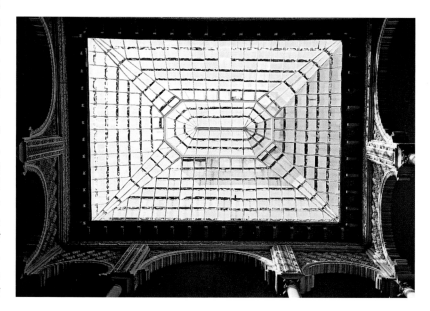

transmission of heat and the insulation of the glazing are improved. This can be further enhanced by a barely visible coating of metallic oxides, usually applied on one inside leaf of double-glazing, to create low-emissivity or 'low-E' glass. This has the property of reflecting the heat from infrared light back into the room, rather like a Thermos flask.

Other treatments variously reduce the transmission of heat and light. Blue, green, bronze or (generally preferable) neutral tinted glass reduce sunlight, although the somewhat darker appearance of the building that results may not be acceptable. Other clear coatings are opaque to ultraviolet light, which reduces the bleaching and tanning effects of sunlight. Further glass coatings, opaque to all but the visible spectrum, significantly reduce the room's heating in bright light, partially removing the need for sun blinds.

In additon to its extraordinary functional qualities, glass is a highly decorative material. Conservatories of the nineteenth century, in which appearance often took precedence over function, featured coloured, etched and crystal glass, often made up in leaded lights, in the smaller panes of fanlights and at the sides of doors. Leaded lights are still incorporated in contemporary conservatories. They are produced by cutting out clear, obscure or coloured glass in small pieces. These are assembled over a full-sized drawing of the design with cut and soldered lead or, occasionally, fine brass jointing pieces called 'cames'. In modern conservatories, such construction works best when the individual pieces of glass are kept small and their colours limited. Glass is available in only a small range of colours, and does not always harmonize to create good colour schemes. A combination of clear and blue glass alone, for example, will work better than trying to use a combination of all the available colours – including deep reds and purple, lots of yellows and ambers, intense greens, pale mauves and pale blue, plus a deep, traditional 'Bristol' blue. A refinement to glass used in leaded lights involves coating ordinary glass with a thin layer, or 'flashing', of

Right: A large conservatory with a lantern roof is wrapped around an existing house chimney. A side conservatory links the kitchen to the space. Although the exterior is designed in a straightforward, greenhouse style, the interior has a sophisticated decorative scheme.

Heating and Cooling

There will not be room for conventional panel radiators in the majority of conservatories, but heating is most effective if positioned on the outer, colder walls, generally under windows. Built-in radiators, set behind panels and containing grilles or louvres at both top and bottom, are effective when placed around a traditional, formal conservatory. Especially successful is heating located in a grille-covered channel set around the perimeter of the floor. This has an appropriate style for a garden room, as it takes up no living space and can raise the temperature quickly through purpose-made, high-output, finned pipes in the channel. The grilles, cast in decorative, pierced patterns, are best made of cast iron, bronze or aluminium (which is suitable for stove-enamelled coloured finishes) and edged with a flush, brass trim. This type of heating creates lots of steam if the channel is watered, aiding the growth of hot-house plants.

Another underfloor heating system works rather like an electric blanket. An electric cable or flexible hot-water pipe snakes back and forth under the floor screed (finished in stone and terracotta, not wood or plastic). This most unobtrusive form of heating gently warms the floor, which in turn heats the room, but the channel system is more responsive and achieves a higher output.

It is usual practice to connect conservatory central heating into the main domestic system. Separate flow and return pipes and independent controls enable the conservatory to be heated separately from the house – for example, at night when warmth is still needed for plants. Wood stoves may supply supplementary heat but, unless an existing flue can be used, a stainless steel insulated flue pipe approximately 30 cm (12 in) in diameter will be required.

Left: A windowsill is needed to cover the top of a stone or brick base, making a useful shelf for plants. On a timber base, or for an extra wide shelf, brackets will be needed; and for full-scale plant staging, the shelf should be of unpainted timber slats.

Right: The corner of the nineteenth-century orangery at Somerleyton Hall, Suffolk has flower beds against the wall and stone plant containers set at intervals. These are lined up with grilles for underfloor heating and for 'damping down' the plants.

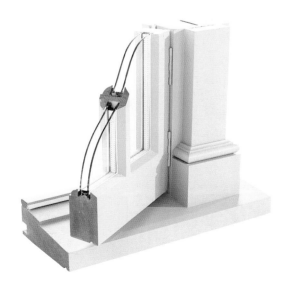

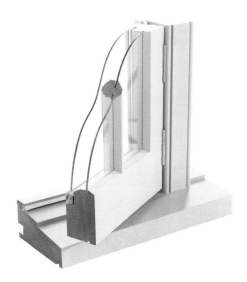

Far left: This is a section of timber construction with individual-sealed double-glazing units. The upright demonstrates framework embellished with pilasters on moulded blocks.

Left: An alternative, simpler style of timber construction is single-glazed for thin dividing bars, with timber-framed secondary glazing fitted inside.

Left: For a bigger roof, electric blinds make sense. They are easy to use and require no hanging cords. The motors are usually barely visible, creating a neat appearance.

Below: A fan lazily turning in the roof, creating a gentle breeze, is a must for sunny conservatories. This example is made especially for conservatories constructed from painted cast iron.

Effective insulation has dramatically improved the efficiency of conservatory heating. The high quality of float glass in turn made sealed-unit double-glazing feasible. This consists of two pieces of glass held apart by a strip of folded metal set around the edge, and then covered externally with polysulphide mastic. The mastic sets moderately hard and, in the right conditions, seals out moisture for over twenty years. However, the ability of mastic to resist the migration of air in and out of the unit, as the air pressure rises and

falls during the day, is seriously reduced at high humidity, resulting in airborne moisture condensing inside the sealed unit. So, unless the unit is either sealed watertight around the perimeter into a frame or fixed into a free-draining channel, the effective life of the glazing will be greatly reduced. Sealed units must be installed to a precise procedure by trained glaziers.

Good ventilation is essential even in the coolest location, unless a glass building is fully sealed and air conditioned. Ventilation works on the simple principle of allowing air to enter low down and, as it warms and rises, to escape high up. This is achieved with openable windows, doors which hook back and, best of all, ventilators built into the ridge of the roof which can be aided with a fan. Ventilators should be generously sized, neatly made so that they do not detract from the lines of the building, and easy to operate. Internal and external shading with blinds, which may be made from fabrics, pinoleum, wood or even metal for outdoor use (see page 133), helps to control the build-up of heat.

Right: Coloured Roman blinds with a woven striped binding and braided cotton cords make an attractive finishing touch. They can be used for privacy as well as shade.

Left: Cedar Venetian blinds, although unsuited to roofs, are a smart choice for doors and windows in city conservatories.

Outside Colour

The role of colour in architecture is often underrated, an afterthought to settle with the decorator. For conservatories, which are largely painted, choosing the right colours is especially important, not least because with modern, long-life paint systems it is not practical to brush on another coat quickly if you want to change the shade. It is better to consider the colour (or, rather, colours, because they are never seen in isolation) from the beginning as part of the design process. Colour decisions should take account of the surrounding buildings and garden, the amount of sun the conservatory will receive, the visual impact it should have, the practicality of maintenance and, not least, local tradition and fashion. Traditionally, conservatories have been white, a colour inherited from greenhouses, which historically were finished with utilitarian white-lead paint. In contemporary paint ranges, however, colour has little relevance to durability or price.

The exterior colour used to paint a conservatory does not have to be used for the interior, and normally the outside colour will only be visible from inside if doors or windows are folded back (the exception being conservatories with deep projections or L-shaped plans, where parts of a building's exterior can be seen clearly). However, the interior colour scheme, including walls, framework, blinds and furniture, will be visible from the outside and must be borne in mind when choosing paint. This is also true of adjacent natural materials – surrounding walls and, in particular, brick or stone base walls and the paving, terracing and nearby planting or trees – which should also influence colour decisions. For example, I once designed a rather large conservatory, and, to minimize its impact, we built it at the end of the house surrounded by mature copper beech trees. We painted the building a beautiful, subtle bronze, a shade taken from the colour of the foliage.

Climate, season and location affect colour, modifying its intensity and shade. As a result, it is important when making a colour selection to view samples of the paint outside, preferably painting them on a board, well in advance. You can then live with the colours for a while, observing them at different times of day and in different weather conditions. It is surprising (as anyone who has attempted to import tropical colours into a temperate setting will tell you) just how much colours change. Even quite dark colours are much more vivid than they usually appear in sunlight if the paint has been mixed using an intense pigment. Generally, light shades have most impact, attracting attention and emphasizing a building's size, while dark colours reduce impact and give greater transparency – it is easier to see through a window divided into small panes if it is not brightly painted.

There is not an ugly colour, only an ugly colour combination, as Dorothy Parker once said, so if the conservatory is built on low stone walls, pick a colour for the paintwork to harmonize perfectly with the stone. Consider whether the exterior should be painted

Left: This colour scheme, centred on soft greens and vibrant mauves and lilac, combines well with the floor and, equally importantly, complements the colours of the planting inside and outside the conservatory.

Below: The bold architectural scale of a conservatory in Hanover is played down with juniper-green paintwork which melts into the surrounding autumn foliage.

'The colours of earth and landscape, of stone and sky, are natural choices for the exterior paintwork of garden rooms.'

in two or even three colours. In this way, the strong architectural qualities of the building can be emphasized, perhaps picking out the framework in a slightly darker shade than the doors and windows, or using colour to highlight decorative brackets, a cornice or roof decoration. Even for a white conservatory there are situations in which the roof should be painted differently, for example slate grey to correspond with an adjoining slate-roofed stucco house. And last, choose a finish for the metal fittings, normally manufactured in brass, which co-ordinates well – either polished brass or finished bronze, satin chrome or bright nickel.

A city conservatory attached to a loft, or on a roof, might be brilliantly coloured, but for most conservatories colours that carry associations with the garden are the most successful. Brick and stone suggest earth colours – umbers, siennas and ochre – while foliage invites soft greens, bronze or greenish-brown. These work well together with greys or blue-greys, which pick up on the colours of water or the sky. Although brilliant white can be harsh, especially in full sunlight, off-white, ivory, parchment and similar shades are easy on the eye and have a smart, contemporary appeal. Wherever you live, there will be colours that are associated with the area, with its own conventions. There may, for example, be a local tradition of painting windows and their frames in separate colours, and then using another colour altogether for the entrance door. Make a conscious decision either to follow the local style or, as the conservatory is a quite different type of construction, to use different paint colours deliberately.

As a general rule, avoid strident colours that you might later regret, and resist transient fashionable combinations that will quickly appear dated. A conservatory is an important, lasting feature and exterior paint colours are not easy to change on a whim; it is preferable to experiment with colours for the interior, which can be replaced more easily. If in doubt, the general impression can be gauged from colouring copies of the design with crayons or watercolours.

Conservatory paints

Although varnishes and stains are occasionally used for the purpose, paint is usually the best finish for timber conservatory structures. The most successful types are generally low-gloss paints that have a high pigment content. These will impart a depth and intensity of colour to the outside of the building, and are environmentally friendly.

There are few regulations or commercial standards that are applied to paints and varnishes. Typically, manufacturers do not provide lists of ingredients and often use misleading marketing terms, such as 'micro-porous', which is a property of all paints in varying degrees. In fact, they all consist of a binder containing pigment in varying amounts that adheres to a surface and hardens. Clear varnishes have no pigment at all, while transparent pigments are present in stains, and

Above: The colour scheme for this conservatory built on Cotswold stone is Portland white. The framework and roof are emphasized by using slate blue. Architectural elements can be reinforced or framed by painting them separately in a palette of two or three colours.

Opposite: The bronze and green exterior helps assimilate this conservatory into the environment of dark timber and tiled buildings. Inside there is a bold shift of shade to delicate pastel greens.

opaque pigments are used in paint. The principle of a preparation that sticks to the surface to which it is applied is common to all three materials. Paint, varnish and stain all require regular refinishing at intervals of between two to ten years (most typically three to five), depending on the location of the building, the qualities of the timber and the finish used.

Traditionally, most paints consisted of a mixture of white and red lead oxide, combined with various minerals and pigments and then ground together with linseed oil. An oxidizing agent was added so that the paint would harden reasonably quickly when exposed to the air. These paints are now largely banned because of their dangerous lead content. Modern alternatives to the older types include polyurethane varnishes and paints, which are mostly used to achieve a high-gloss finish. Lead paint was eventually replaced by alkyd paint, a material that has increased in quality substantially in recent years. This has achieved comparable durability to lead paint, and high-quality versions, designed specifically for the purpose of finishing or repainting exterior woodwork, are now produced by many manufacturers.

The second group of paints that are suitable for conservatories consists of water-based resins. The addition of water to the mix makes application easy, quick and possibly safer. Although the qualities of water-based paints have been much improved, a full gloss finish still cannot be achieved. Acrylic paints, manufactured from combinations of acrylic resins and pigment, are preferable for outside use. The best quality acrylic, with superior ingredients in the right quantities, is expensive, but is often worth the inital outlay because it offers the greatest durability – up to ten years before a further coat is needed. Vinyl paints are only suitable for use inside the conservatory. Always use the best quality paint available, as price is insignificant compared to the cost of preparing and applying it.

Above: A dramatic colour scheme of inky blue outside and white with terracotta inside, to match the house roof, has been devised for this conservatory.

Exterior Paint

Paint modifies our perception of shape and structure: it can dramatically change the visual impact of a building, making it seem more or less modest or grand, rustic or sleek. Dark colours give a sense of increased transparency to the framing, while a two-tone scheme will have the opposite effect. Good modern paints are usually water-based.

Right: A gentle colour is chosen to soften the architectural features of a conservatory set in a flower garden.

Far right: At the initial planning stage, the colour scheme here was resolved not just for the building, but also for the interior design, furniture, surrounding garden and plants, to create a bold integrated effect.

Right: White paintwork will emphasize the scale and importance of a conservatory in its setting, and it should be used in a considered way for a dramatic effect.

Far right: In an urban environment, white paintwork is all too often soiled. For a lantern roof that is difficult to reach, a coloured finish is a more practical choice.

Left: Olive green is used here for the paintwork so that the structure will blend with walls of local Gloucestershire stone.

Right: Earth colours suggesting stonework are a good choice for an orangery-style construction with timber columns.

4

Linking with the Garden

A successful conservatory is one that is designed with sensitivity to the surrounding landscape. The first orangeries were conceived as one element in a harmonious garden plan encompassing avenues, terraces, balustrades and fountains. The elegant raised buildings that form the conservatory at Syon House near London, for example, open on to a terrace decorated with carved urns to match the classical sandstone façade. Several steps lead down to a formal garden with views towards a pool beyond. On a smaller scale, correspondences between the conservatory and a well-composed garden or terrace can also make the difference between an attractive and an undistinguished design. The outside world is always on display in a consevatory, in which large glass walls function as picture windows, and any incoherent elements will disturb the overall look. It is wise to identify any problems in the landscape or aspect at the planning stage of the conservatory, as not only individual features but the gradient and perspective can more easily be modified at this stage. Nonetheless, start from a principle of working with, rather than against, the setting, reflecting the best aspects of its character in the new building's design.

Opposite: This conservatory and garden were planned and built together to extend a Princeton, USA home. A strong symmetry – and carefully proportioned steps descending to paths leading to a garden pavilion – combine to create a balanced and attractive scene.

The Great Outdoors

The setting of any new building can make the difference between architectural success and failure, but this is especially true of a conservatory. In this suspended space, poised between house and garden, the view from inside is as important as the outside appearance, and distinctions are softened between interior and exterior worlds. Conservatories should not be conceived in isolation: most are an addition to an existing building on an established site. The compromises needed to integrate new with old make it easy to neglect the surrounding garden, yet its style and shape, the plants, walls and neighbouring buildings, must also be accommodated in the overall design. A successful conservatory leads the living space out into the garden beyond, ideally connected by large glazed doors and a convenient terrace.

The conservatory is often used rather like a marquee, to provide a garden base for eating and entertaining. Half indoors, half out, it offers shelter from breezes or cooler weather, extending the clemency of spring and autumn. Some space immediately outside the doors is useful, whether it is a formal terrace or a small area of paving. A barbecue may be grilled outside on the terrace, but served in the comfort of the open conservatory with the doors and windows wide. I always recommend large, outward-opening doors, with hinges that allow them to be hooked back for ventilation and proximity to the garden. The position of the doors will, in part, be dictated by the furniture layout, but if they can align with the internal doors to adjacent rooms, you may enjoy an uninterrupted view of the conservatory and garden beyond from, say, the living room. In places where it gets especially hot in summer, such as Spain and parts of America, air conditioning may be desirable, but conservatories should be cool for much of the year if open to the garden, and assisted by sun-shading, insulating glass and, perhaps, a fan. Depending on the locality, insect screens may help; these are best designed as part of the structure to blend attractively into the fabric of the building.

Capturing the sun

In a sunny location, a sun-trap for relaxing and entertaining can often be created next to a conservatory. It is best constructed at the same level as the conservatory floor to minimize the boundaries between inside and outside and make it easier to carry furniture to and fro. It should also be sheltered, partly by the building itself, but also by trees, hedges or walls, which will also add a degree of privacy. In such an arrangement, you may well find yourself needing two sets of tables and chairs for eating, according to occasion and season. To add variety, one can be round and the other square or rectangular, and each can be made from different materials. Outside, there is a more limited choice and some of the furniture will need to be put away or protected in bad weather. A convenient store nearby for cushions is important; chairs may be stored there in winter, but a table will probably be kept permanently outside,

Right: A formal, orangery-style garden room designed by Richard Heelas of Marston & Langinger for a villa in Antwerp. The building incorporates a large terrace of doors which open down to both the lawn and the terrace.

Below: Outside, the bold lines of this substantial poolhouse are softened with informal planting and steps tumbling down to an adjoining lake.

requiring washing to control mould. Bleach is effective, but may damage the material. A good alternative is fungicides used for horticulture; they should be applied to the table at the end of the season.

Raised or sunken conservatories

Smaller conservatories, especially those on urban sites where space is limited, may not have scope for a full terrace, but the design can still respond imaginatively to the enviornment. Very small conservatories, for example, can be constructed on the balcony over a bay window or portico, or created to form an extra storey to a masonry extension at the side or rear. The close proximity of city living means that architectural coherence with adjacent buildings and garden features are important when building a new addition. Take time to explore a setting's potential before fixing upon the conservatory's size and shape. Even locations that are far from ideal can be adapted to make the best use of the surrounding space.

City houses, especially older ones, often have a change of level downwards from front to back, with the conservatory filling a recess or awkward corner. A sunken courtyard will be needed outside the conservatory to allow room for the doors, if they open outward, to swing back, and for steps up into the garden. This space can either be small and functional or large enough to include a bench or table and chairs. A change of level up to the garden can be partially disguised with grass or planting. This should reduce the vertical masonry visible from inside and greatly improve the view out. Steps up to the garden can be made shallower and wider than is strictly necessary, so that the sides can be used for plants in pots. If the position is sunny, the steps may be used to sit on.

A raised conservatory presents a different set of possibilities. Raising the level of a building makes it more dominant, which may not be appropriate. If this is the case, its impact can be reduced by sloping the ground away from the conservatory, and softening the

Above: The ground level and lawn (photographed in the early mid-winter sun and frost) have been gently graded so that the conservatory is raised up to the level of the house and looks natural in its setting.

Overleaf: The poolhouse linking the conservatory on a beautiful site has been carefully positioned by designer Richard Ross-Harper at Marston & Langinger to make the most of the location, creating fine views both looking out and looking in. The terrace is gently landscaped and planted to assimilate the new building into an old setting.

effect with planting in front of and around the building. A terrace is essential where there are doors, and this will need a balustrade for safety if there is a significant drop from the level of the terrace to the garden.

Although a change in level requires extra planning and design and is more elaborate to construct, it can be looked upon as an exciting opportunity to create interesting spaces and views inside and out. Changing the landscape in this way enables you to develop new living areas, perhaps for breakfast or entertaining in the summer, and for gardening. Considerable earth moving may be needed for the right effect, including construction of a level platform for the conservatory base and terrace. It is not a cheap process: together with steps, walls and foundations, shaping the site may cost as much as the conservatory itself, although results can be well worthwhile. When there is a drop of two metres or more, instead of filling in the space beneath the conservatory, an additional garden store or room can be made – a wine cellar, for example, or even a gym. Earth banks fill in the space around a raised conservatory, with gently rising steps cut into them; they are generally more suited to an open, less urban situation. On a town site, a vertical masonry base with steep stone or cast-iron steps may be needed (cast iron is less noisy underfoot than steel, unless it is especially

Above: Building a conservatory to provide extra space on a restricted city site requires design ingenuity. Here the conservatory is raised up to drawing-room level and the garden is pushed out to make a well-lit basement breakfast room. The design is unified with two sets of doors, each relating to the other, and the change of level is softened by a flower-filled balcony.

Left: A formal approach to the change of level between garden room and lawn is achieved with a wide terrace and broad steps.

Left: The surrounding trees were protected during the construction of this conservatory and left to grow. They help to integrate the new building into the garden environment.

thick). Steps built symmetrically across the front are more imposing than those tucked away at the side. A dramatic alternative is to construct the conservatory a bold two storeys high, and build the staircase between the levels within it.

Using the landscape

It is important to integrate the new conservatory building into the plan of an existing garden. The traditional role of eighteenth-century orangeries was directly linked with the experience of the garden. They were often placed at the end of avenues of trees or where paths crossed, providing elegant diversion or an opportunity for refreshments for those invited to enjoy the pleasures of the extensive grounds. Many such orangeries were positioned in front of trees, especially evergreens, their white paintwork silhouetted against dark foliage. Modern conservatories, particularly those positioned at the rear of town houses, can be painted in a light colour that will brighten a sombre, overshadowed setting.

Location and size are critical factors in blending a conservatory into the outdoor scene. If it will be too dominant in the space, resist the temptation to order too large a building. Incorporating existing features of the garden helps to blur together old and new – a terrace or path anchors the new building visually, as does the thoughtful disposition of containers, hedges and shrubs. Boundary walls in stone or brick are often raised up to become the end wall of a conservatory, which makes good use of space and unifies the addition with the existing plan. However, garden walls are rarely adequate without waterproofing and insulation, and older walls may have no foundations. A solution if the wall is firm is to raise it up to the correct height and dry-line it with an insulating and waterproofing plasterboard, which is then in turn plaster-finished. A more robust method, if the existing wall is weak or the new inside finish will carry many fixings, is to construct a 10 cm- (4in-) thick brick or blockwork wall on the inside – although this uses space that is particularly precious in a city conservatory.

Right: The conservatory fills a gap between two buildings, with a raised-up garden wall behind to create privacy. The terrace and floor have been set at virtually the same level so that in summer the large doors can be folded back and the spaces inside and out used together.

'A clever new conservatory design can give the appearance of being an integral part of the original garden and house plan, blending effortlessly with landscape and architecture.'

The Surrounding Terrace

Whatever the size and scale of a conservatory, it should reflect the influences of house and garden, inside and outside worlds, and needs to make sense within the logic of surrounding features. No matter how well designed and built it is, the conservatory will look awkward and not be fully utilized if it is not married to its setting. It needs appropriate terracing and steps, walls, hedges and other garden features to complete the scene. In a sunny location, there may be further seating and a table outside, or interesting year-round planting that can be appreciated from within the comfort of the conservatory. There may be paths leading off to other parts of the garden, and carefully placed tubs, seats or garden ornaments.

Terraces provide a particularly useful link between garden and conservatory – an additional stage in the transition from enclosed to fully exposed environment. If there is no change in level, large double doors can easily be folded back in warm weather to provide an even and continuous floor between inside and out. This is particularly convenient when carrying food, drinks or furniture. It should be constructed with a break, a very small step or water bar beneath the doors, to keep rainwater out. The terrace will need an external drain, placed within a gully under the paving surface and covered with a cast-iron grille. Water can thus drain safely off the terrace, away from the conservatory floor.

Reflecting the garden design

Domestic gardens often follow similar structural patterns. The more formal aspects, including symmetry, hard surfaces and neatly cut hedges, are placed close to the house, with a more naturalistic planting and trees occurring as you move further into the grounds. This suits the practical needs of a garden, with the terrace acting as an extension of the living space while the less visited rear part of the garden provides the backdrop and view from the terrace and conservatory. The terrace can be defined as an outside room, with low walls or clipped hedges, perhaps under-planted with mind-your-own-business, violets and other ground-cover plants. Small changes of level that occur can easily be accommodated at this point. When a conservatory has low, brick, base walls, the exterior may benefit if narrow beds are created in front of them, planted with low-growing shrubs (in order not to restrict openable windows), such as lavender, box and varieties of rosemary, santolina or euphorbias. If the house is old, planting is a useful way to cover up the new walls until they have mellowed.

The alternative, appropriate for a more naturalistic garden style, is to blur the transition from conservatory to garden. Use a rich mixture of coloured and textured blossom and foliage, including shrubs, climbers and trees, to surround and overhang the conservatory. This is most effective if you are a keen conservatory gardener and adopt the same style across the boundaries of inside and out. Take the chance to experiment with

Right: The terrace between the conservatory and the lawn at the bottom of steps provides an intermediate space, but avoids a sharp change in level.

Opposite: When asked to design a poolhouse by the owners of a nineteenth-century hunting lodge in the Ardennes, my solution was a traditional white conservatory with a balcony and staircases down to a lower garden. All the levels have views of the surrounding woodland and glimpses of the rolling countryside beyond.

exotic plants that can withstand slight frosts and thrive in the somewhat milder city climate: evergreen palms, bananas and tree ferns outside a conservatory serve to emphasize the exciting environment within. These plants often have interesting architectural shapes and provide colour through the year.

Seats or benches, apart from being useful when relaxing or entertaining, provide attractive focal points on the terrace. They can also be used to fill gaps under or between trees. A slab of stone or even a thick plank of oak built into a recess makes a simple and effective bench. Steel or iron furniture is fine used outdoors,

provided that it is galvanized – a handsome, grey zinc finish that prevents rust for many years. It can be over-painted, providing a good opportunity to use interesting or strong colours, developing and extending the colour scheme used inside the conservatory.

The shape and structure of outdoor furniture is important in establishing the atmosphere of the terrace. The sinuous, wrought-iron legs of metal furniture designs echo the delicate forms of surrounding plants. Solid table tops of marble and stone provide sleek, interesting contrasts with the natural textures outdoors, but can be heavy to carry in and out. Wicker furniture

Above: Wirework benches are light and graceful and can be left outside all year round. If they are used in a dark location, they can be brightly painted.

'Terraces, patios and paths are the floors of the garden, and they give an outdoor 'room' coherence and pattern.'

is easy to transport and has a classic feel that works well in a traditional setting. It should always be stored indoors, however, and will need soft cushions.

Paths and paving

Similar flooring materials create useful thematic links between the conservatory and garden environments. The match may not always be easy or immediate: new bricks, stonework and paving will take a few years' exposure to the elements before they blend with existing materials. The difference can be quite dramatic in an old house and garden unless old materials are sourced specifically to reflect those that already exist. The mortar between bricks or stone is equally important. Modern, grey, cement-based mortar will not match old mortar made with lime. It is possible to obtain the latter, but coloured cements mixed with selected sand will do as an alternative. Even the way the mortar is finished depends on its intended use or to match surrounding walls: flush between the bricks or stone, depressed with a slight hollow or struck smoothly at an angle.

Natural stone flags of sandstone or grit, which are inherently non-slip, roughly dressed into squares or rectangles laid in a random pattern, are one of the best choices for paving. They can be placed loosely together with no fall, allowing rainwater to drain through the gaps between them, which should be filled with coarse sand mixed with a very small amount of lime or cement. This not only allows water to drain away, but permits, if desired, small plants such as thyme and saxifrages to creep from the gaps between the flags for an attractive country look. Newer flags made out of accurately cut slabs should be laid with a fall, and, because the joints can be so tight, the gaps filled with cement mortar. Bricks, provided they are constructed as frost-proof paviors rather than house bricks, can be laid attractively, forming squares, diamonds or herringbone patterns, or mixed with flints, granite setts, pebbles or small stone flags. Granite setts, which are

hand-finished usually in 10 cm, 12 cm or 15 cm (4 in, 5 in or 6 in) cubes, make valuable, slip-resistant paving and are especially good for curved or twisting paths. They can also be used as an edging. Cobbles – stones from beaches worn naturally round – may also be used as edgings, or as narrow, winding paths for occasional use. If you are able to obtain cobbles in various colours and sizes, then they can be used to make patterns – not only typical compass shapes, but also petals, overlapping circles, squares or diamonds – set as a decorative feature in the terrace. Although gravel, fine or coarse, normally needs raking and may need to be

Above: Pebblework, although labour intensive, is easily constructed with a well-prepared design. It has a modest charm which complements a conservatory style.

Left: The space outside a conservatory can be particularly inviting – close to the garden, a step away from the house and yet, with doors wide open, within easy reach of the family or refreshments. Here the main garden is only visible through openings in a hedge, which surrounds the conservatory to create an intimate terrace.

removed from shoes or door thresholds, it is excellent for paths when it is rolled and bound to freshly compacted aggregate mixed with sand and lime. It is a useful decorative aid – pale varieties can bring light and colour into a dark shaded area of the terrace. Gravel does tend to drift, however, and needs a firm edging of bricks or setts.

The terrace garden

In creating a garden for a terrace, as for a conservatory, it is important to consider the daily patterns of light and shade. Dark corners can be enlivened with shade-loving foliage plants, while the sunniest areas may need a canvas shade – or tall planting. Less movable but of more long-term benefit is a permanent pergola, constructed from trellis or wire and festooned in summer with climbers, such as honeysuckle, clematis or roses. Foliage and flowers serve to soften hard angles, or to divide up an open area, on a terrace.

I have never been able to resist growing collections of plants in pots on terraces. Personally I prefer to see a terrace decorated with beautiful plants in fine, hand-thrown pots rather than with statuary, despite the high maintenance of container-grown plants. There is an inevitable conflict when choosing plants between the aesthetic logic of garden design and the enthusiasm to try out new varieties and build collections of plants. A cluster of assorted plants is unlikely to have the visual impact of, say, a line of spiky cordylines, which in turn are much less rewarding close up. This dilemma can be resolved on a formal terrace by first choosing bold evergreen perennials to emphasize the lines of the terrace garden, and then adding interest with a variety of flowering plants that can be moved according to season. Position each of them prominently as they reach their best, to ensure that the view from the conservatory is rewarding throughout the year. Good choices are spring bulbs and lilies, which can be moved in their pots to recover in a quiet corner of the garden after their flowering season is over.

Leafy climbers, such as actinidia, a grape vine, honeysuckle or ivy, relieve the harshness of brick or cement-finished walls, and will easily cover pipes. The blooms of flowering species, typically roses and wisteria, look beautiful through a glass roof. Established trees close by are an asset, providing a canopy of foliage and useful shade. With toughened new glass, only larger branches are likely to cause damage. Trees can be used to harmonize the general aspect from inside the conservatory, cover unsightly views and ensure privacy.

Garden pools normally tend to be built some way off from the house, perhaps through concerns over safety, algae or insects. However, a simple, shallow, rectangular pool with vertical sides can be easy to look after and reasonably safe. Oxygenation or oxygenating plants, together with suitable breeds of fish, will keep it clear and reasonably free of insects. Through its movement and reflections, a pool adds a cool, sensual element to the terrace design, and can be positioned to reflect the inverted silhouette of the conservatory. If it is constructed with a liner, the top can be covered with an edging of stone and the bottom with large, black pebbles. Smaller pools generally work best with one or two clumps of the same plant. For example, try a single

Right: In the summer months, the boundary between living areas inside and out becomes blurred by an assortment of pots, tables and chairs.

large clump of cyperus – tall, green stalks with fans of spikes on top – or arum lilies with lush, arrow-point leaves and white trumpet flowers.

A conservatory roof can help to provide water for the plants growing inside and on the terrace. This is particularly useful in hard-water districts, especially if you are growing plants such as citrus varieties, camellias and gardenias, which thrive in a lime-free environment. Rainwater should be drained into a container with an overflow leading to a drain; a tight-fitting lid is essential to keep out insects, including mosquitos, as well as leaves. Second-hand oak butts are reasonably priced and attractive, and can be set on bricks in a corner of the terrace. They do require routine creosoting, however, while more expensive lead tanks, often decorated with beautiful patterns, do not need maintenance. Provided that the storage container is set high enough, a pipe may be taken from the bottom through and into the conservatory for convenient indoor watering. In winter, however, water taken straight from the tap may be close to freezing, causing shock to plants in a heated environment. Allow the water to warm indoors before putting it to use.

Garden ornament on a terrace will strengthen the sense of it as an outdoor room. Urns, classical vases, statues and even antique chimney-pots can be used on a formal terrace to define corners, steps and openings to paths. Typical materials are salt-glazed earthenware – which is frost-proof – lead, cast iron – which generally needs painting – and stone or bronze for statuary. Urns set on plinths or tall chimney-pots can be planted with ornamental trailing ivy, agapanthus, agave and sempervivum – all plants that are able to cope with summer heat.

To make full use of the terrace, outdoor lighting is essential. As with lighting indoors, a myriad of dancing small flames has far more magic than harsh security lamps. Chinese lanterns, or nightlights in hanging coloured-glass holders, are good for a party, while flares are dramatic, although they tend to drip and to smoke.

Left: In the confined space of a town garden, it is usually better to avoid grass and pave the central area so that it can be used for furniture, leaving a margin of the garden around the boundaries.

5

Interior Style

Glass rooms with their architectural quality created by high roofs and exposed structural features provide an exciting opportunity for interior decoration in styles not possible elsewhere in the house. Other rooms in the home are constructed of brick and concrete, with steelwork and sawn woodwork joists and framing encased in plaster, trimmed with architraves, skirtings and decoration. The structure of a glasshouse, however, is entirely visible from inside and out: the structure is itself the decoration, and vice versa. The proximity of the world outside and the view of the garden, terrace, plants, trees and the surroundings should influence the materials, colours and textures used indoors, and reflect an awareness of the constantly changing seasons outside. Even in the most elegantly dressed room, a sense of informality and leisure is important, balanced with the comfort of soft fabrics and a subtle lighting scheme.

Opposite: The wicker furniture, with its natural, rustic associations, is softened in this elegant yet practical interior scheme with glorious lilac cushions and delicate, floor-length voile curtains.

Dressing the Space

Because the conservatory is closely associated with the outside world, its interior decoration and furnishing should draw first from this theme. Garden room interiors can reflect materials and textures from outdoors, adapted and reinterpreted within a warm and comfortable setting. Mellow old brick and stone walls, for example, can be filled and sealed but left unplastered. The floor may be old stone flags or rough brick, but damp-proofed so that a rug may be put down in winter. Furniture and decoration may contain similar resonances from the garden scene; a peeling antique bench, dressed with pretty new cushions, for example, may be put against the wall and mossy old garden pots planted up and arranged on a table. Even lighting is influenced by the exterior world, with lanterns, candles and decorative oil lamps contributing to the overall mood of a room. Above all, conservatories are very personal places in which imagination and individual preference can interpret the needs and features of a particular setting; what suits a conservatory adjoining a fifteenth-century farmhouse might strike a false note on a modern city roof top.

The interior colour scheme should flow in from the natural surroundings, reflecting the earth colours of stone and brick, the subtle variations of foliage and the brilliant concentrations of flower colours. Neutral colours (black, white and greys) together with natural browns, rusts, creams and off-whites often form the basis of a conservatory scheme; contrasting details and accents balance the warmth and coolness of the look. The natural palette contains wide variations of tone and hue, allowing the creation of subtle and effective

Left: The quirky interior of sculptor Andrew Logan's glasshouse home uses brilliant colour to draw attention to the individual spaces within the large room.

Right: Designer Sue Timney used a full-width conservatory of a simple lean-to shape to create the most used space of her London home – a combined kitchen, dining and day room. The strongly individualistic style combines slate flooring and slate-grey framing with natural timber walls and furniture, reflecting her interest in Arts and Crafts design.

Far left: A large antique mirror, seasonally draped with dried hops, fills the space behind a sofa and balances the solid and glazed walls.

Left: Mirrors compensate for solid walls in a garden room by reflecting light, glass and greenery. The mirror and fireplace utilize the somewhat awkward space between two sets of doors at the back of the conservatory.

Above: Soft pastels, comfortable loungers and a pretty view induce tranquillity in this conservatory, used as an attractive sitting room.

Right: The interior of this conservatory, built to suit a Victorian Gothic mansion, is furnished with natural teak to complement a brick and stone floor and original brick walls.

combinations consistent with the outdoor theme. Remember that colours are never perceived in isolation, but always in the context of those around them, and that daylight will change individual hues, depending on season and time of day. Natural colours generally work well together, however, and will bring a sense of calm to the garden room.

The texture of materials plays an important role in shaping the design, particularly as it modifies colour, adding subtlety and variation. In order to be practical, conservatory surfaces need to be robust, with easily maintained finishes (matt and textured rather than highly polished). This works well for authentic, rustic materials – wicker, unvarnished wood, sisal and jute, linen and cotton. These have a straightforward, relaxing honesty fitting for a garden room, yet also a rough edge which prevents a natural, mellow scheme from becoming bland. Matt finishes are particularly effective in a bright, light room, where too much reflection would be uncomfortable.

Floors constitute the largest single block of colour in most conservatories, a role usually filled by the solid walls of a conventional room. The colour and markings of natural floor surfaces are part of their character and effect, and there is often great variety found within a single material (see pages 70–71). Where possible, seek to echo the flooring of a terrace or patio outside, but always consider the effect of stone or brick colours in the context of the whole room.

In a conservatory timber floors will split and erode in sunlight; use it instead in an unrefined way, without tight joints or varnish. However, wood makes an attractive finish, either in panels that unify solid and glazed areas or as match-boarding reminiscent of beach huts and sports pavilions. Brick or blockwork walls should be finished with cement-based masonry paint or traditional lime paints, available in beautiful, rich colours, rather than smooth vinyl-emulsion painted plaster. Remember that internal walls are exposed, so colours should harmonize with the outside setting.

'Stripes are a classic pattern for garden-room fabric.
They make a good background for smaller pillows to
introduce accents of bright colour.'

Left: Feather or synthetic down-filled seat cushions, on wicker furniture with plenty of pretty scatters, complement the masculinity of the architecture in this conservatory to create a balanced, comfortable room.

Conservatory furniture

Asked to suggest typical conservatory furniture, most of us would immediately propose wicker, whether in sofas, ottomans, tables or chairs. The material has been popular throughout the nineteenth and twentieth centuries because of its practical, informal nature and attractive associations of living in the garden or on the veranda. Wicker's appeal lies in its essential simplicity, and it remains an excellent material today, adapting to current fashion for classic designs with a natural or matt-painted finish and the addition of loose cushions.

Wicker is versatile, authentic in feel and resistant to heat, humidity and direct sunlight. It is also the perfect 'green' material. Entirely handmade from various waterside plants – willow, rattan and osier – it is grown without fertilizers and harvested by cutting shoots, or 'withes', each summer, leaving the plant to regenerate for the next season. The withes are soaked and are woven into chairs, sofas and tables; the tops must be even if they are to provide practical surfaces. Wicker furniture is best used indoors or outdoors on a veranda, but painted wicker can occasionally be left on an open terrace. Though light and easy to move, it can be bulky and always needs cushions. Painted wicker is more honed and sophisticated in style, and can be used to provide a striking contrast in a sleek urban conservatory. Natural wicker is used occasionally with its brown rustic look, but more usually this is stripped to leave a smooth buff finish which may also be bleached creamy-white.

Conservatory tables require materials that are robust and do not suffer from damp or sunlight, and they should be chosen together with chairs as part of a unified design. Unvarnished wood is attractive, and old oak or chestnut work well; teak is widely used outside but is rarely successful indoors. A base made of new, painted pine can be combined with a stone top, but the classic choice for table bases is iron. Strong, light and adaptable, iron can be worked into attractive shapes, painted or given a natural-looking waxed finish to reflect light. It is also 'see-through' in the sense that the legs and components are slim but barely interrupt the view, echoing the framework's transparency. Slender and elegant wire trellis, jardinières, hanging baskets and chandeliers contribute to this.

Table surfaces need to be smooth to be practical, and slate, stone, marble and glass meet this requirement without being too glitzy. Slate – usually black Welsh, grey-green Cumbrian or green Italian – looks good and is especially strong. Sandstone needs to be thick and is quite heavy, and should be used to create a monumental look. Limestone cannot normally be cut big enough for tabletops, although marble is regularly available. Scagliola is a surprisingly durable imitation marble made by mixing coloured plasters, which when hard

Above: An Indonesian rattan lounger and a footstool provide comfort in a sunny corner of a tall, architecturally bold, bronze-coloured orangery.

Below: Iron furniture, with its light, open framework, suits the transparent construction of a conservatory, but cushions are an essential addition.

Interior Colour Schemes

Released from the design constraints imposed by the exterior, and from the conventions of drawing or dining room, the conservatory can be different and individual. The colours used here will have a unique quality because of the brilliant natural light within the room.

Below: A subtle touch of orange lifts this warm, masculine combination of red-coloured lime plaster, floor of Cambridge paviors, natural oak and wicker furniture and deep bronze-green woodwork.

Above: Although logically you would expect to see growing, rather than cut, flowers arranged in a conservatory, these look pretty as part of a table setting made up of intense summer colours.

Above: The primulas in the foreground, grown in pots on the terrace, are chosen for their brilliant colour, which picks up on the spring colours, mauve with green, of the interior. The huge four-seater sofa is set into a snug recess.

Overleaf: Stripes seem the natural choice in a garden room. A bench upholstered with a woven stripe by Susan Hirsh makes a cosy corner. The windowsill has a wire plant pot holder, and an antique Royal Doulton water cooler is used for a Cymbidium orchid. A scented geranium on the right has fern-like, finely-divided leaves.

Combining Colours and Textures

The recipe for a successful colour scheme depends not only on the selection, but also on the intensity and the mix of the ingredients. The effect also depends on whether surface textures in the scheme reflect or absorb light. The swatches below illustrate some classic garden-room combinations.

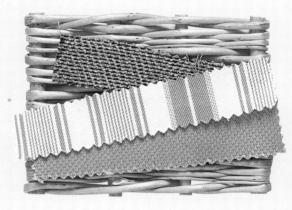

The diverse Marston & Langinger fabrics shown here are chosen to harmonize or contrast, through both colour and texture, with the different wicker samples beneath. It is important also to remember that the colours of fabrics will not be perceived in isolation, but as part of the overall palette of the building and its surroundings. The colours chosen for the room will also appear different in shade and in full sunlight, and under artificial light in the evening.

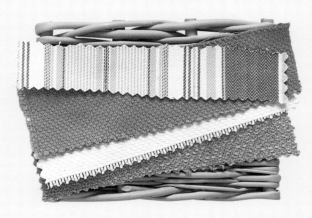

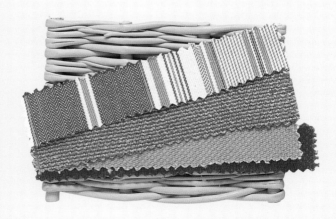

The Tiger Rugs of Tibet

100 KILIMS

YANNI PETSOPOULOS

'Soft furnishings assume a whole new identity in the garden room – one that speaks of comfort and relaxed, outdoor living.'

are smoothed, oiled and waxed. A brilliant imitation of natural material, it gives great scope for creativity. Other, unusual finishes used as a covering to timber are lead, zinc or copper. Glass is lighter and can be frosted, etched or beveled, but it scratches easily and needs care. Various mosaics – glass, stone or Moroccan glazed earthenware – can be successful, depending on the mosaic maker's skill as an artist. Painted iron has the charm of old, French café furniture and, being light, is good for small tables that need to be moved around.

Suitable dining chairs to go with these tables generally fall between garden and dining chairs in style.

Mostly metal, cast aluminium or steel, they are usually either painted or given a polished or waxed black finish. Wirework is attractive, wicker (though bulky) can be comfortable and Lloyd Loom designs are a possibility. Although often bought separately, chairs and tables should balance one another and co-ordinate with the design overall.

Soft furnishings and fabrics

Conservatories should not be dressed in the same way as a reception room, with curtain treatments that would obscure the framework of the building or with heavily

Above: Side blinds can be left down permanently for privacy. Made from pinoleum, these eliminate seventy-five per cent of the light to leave finely-patterned shadows.

upholstered sofas. However, soft furnishings and fabrics play an important role in the design. They enhance colour and texture, make the room comfortable and cosy at night or in winter, and are valuable finishing touches. A conservatory uses different textiles from those in the rest of the house: they must be made with colour-fast dyes that are able to cope with direct sunlight. Unassuming, practical materials such as linen and cotton (of the kind that might also be used outdoors) are the most appropriate, with coarse, wild silk a glamorous but less hardwearing option. Made from renewable materials, they are natural companions for stonework, wood and wicker.

Woven stripes, including ticking, and checks are also fabrics that traditionally find their place in the garden room. Stripes and checks mix well together when each uses colours that echo or complement the surrounding paintwork, and they can be mixed with corresponding one-colour fabrics. Floral-printed cotton and linen occasional cushions work well when teamed with woven-pattern upholstery. Coarse canvas and linens, including cushion covers of cut-down antique linen, suit a weathered, traditional interior style.

Very few conservatories receive no sunlight at all: so control of the sun is essential. Even in winter, midday sun will quickly build up heat in the room, while in summer it will be relentless. Although coatings can be

applied to the glass, these will be tinted or reflective unless a premium price is paid. Consequently, blinds will be needed, which also soften the lines of the room, provide privacy if needed, and serve to make the room cosier in winter. Highly efficient sun blinds (see page 133), can be relieved by decorative, softer blinds fitted around the windows. Delicately coloured cotton voile curtains (see page 109) can be suspended in soft folds from rings on a metal rod. Coarse, coloured flax sacking, plain or striped, with matching flax ties done up in bows is another garden room approach. Pinoleum with pretty, striped edges, on rollers or hung Roman fashion,

Left: This combined kichen and living room interior is illuminated with a pair of magnificent eighteenth-century candelabras. Behind them, set into the soffit, are miniature, low-voltage starlights, which are controlled by a dimmer to complement the candlelight.

'Lighting a garden room that has few solid surfaces but seemingly acres of glass requires a special artistry.'

has a neater, more restrained appearance. Such curtains and blinds have a suitable style, and should be selected with the colours and texture of the room. I have not covered full-scale, lined curtains, valances or pelmets, as these are more suited to windows of conventional rooms beyond the scope of this book. It is worth noting that light shining through blinds will be modified and slightly tinted by the colour of the fabric.

Lighting the conservatory

Glass rooms present particular lighting problems, as a building designed to let light in will also let much of it out. There is very little soft, reflected background light due to the lack of solid ceilings and other painted surfaces; and because the spread of individual lamps is relatively small, more are needed for even illumination than would be the case in other rooms of the house. Lighting arrangements that suit most domestic rooms thus need to be modified in a conservatory. Uplighters,

for example, are not effective, as most of the light is lost through the glass and the rest bounces back as sharp reflections from roof panes. The solution is to use both fixed roof and side lighting, as well as plug-in side and table lamps, hanging lamps and chandeliers. A variety of low-intensity lamps, including some associated with outdoor use, is more successful than a few bright ones, which will cause glare. Starlights, wall brackets, oil lamps, lanterns and candles enhance the conservatory's natural atmosphere and make practical use of the space.

The tall ceilings of conservatories provide a perfect setting for low-voltage halogen star lamps. Available in very small sizes (operated in a group by a concealed transformer), they work excellently in a timber roof, recessed unobtrusively into the main beams. Starlights give even, high-quality background light, showing colours accurately. Wall lights are often best in their simplest form – plain glass lamps with decorative brass brackets easily fixed to the framing.

Far left: Although interior light will flood through on to the terrace, specific outside lighting is essential if the area is to be used at night.

Left: Traditional lanterns in zinc – or copper, as here – or painted ones do not have the output of security lamps, but beat them hands down for appearance.

Outdoor lights illuminate a terrace or paths around the conservatory, and they admit additional light into the room. Garden lanterns with a soft glow are thus preferable to harsh security lights. A range of authentic fittings can be attached to areas of the external framework below the gutter; they may be functional and inconspicuous or decorative features.

Standard or table lamps provide the main source of low-level conservatory lighting. These may be similar to those elsewhere in the house, although adjustable arms for task lighting are particularly important, given the lower level of background light. Choosing the correct size and style of shade for a table lamp is essential, as it affects how light radiates – reflected up or down, glowing behind a translucent shade or focused on to a specific point. Both forms of lamp can be plugged into a circuit controlled by a switch to avoid operating them manually – a dimmer switch is ideal.

Hanging lamps, unfashionable in reception rooms, are very effective suspended from high conservatory

Above: A chandelier, prettified with loops of cut-glass beads and hanging pendants, adds sparkle to a refined interior.

Left: Antique lamps are perfect in conservatories, but check that they are properly wired.

'The romance of a chandelier or of flickering candlelight cannot be eclipsed by the march of modern technology.'

Left: The central chandelier is electrified with tiny candle-flame bulbs. In the background, electric reproductions of eighteenth-century oil lamps fit well in the garden room.

Right: A central, hanging glass lantern is chosen to echo the materials and structure of the conservatory it illuminates.

Far right: I based the design of this lamp on a Turkish kiosk pattern, with wire sides and perforated patterns that are projected on to surrounding surfaces by the bulbs.

roofs. A traditional rise-and-fall lamp is perfect over a table. Simple fittings with globe or prismatic-glass shades provide good general lighting in a larger space. All kinds of decorative lanterns may be hung in a garden room, reinforcing the sense of the outdoor environment. Many modern attractive lanterns are based on traditional oil or candle lamps of Moorish, Turkish or Coptic styles. Oil lamps are practical and somehow more charming the cheaper they are. Once a feature of nineteenth-century conservatories, they can today be fuelled with odourless paraffin, which is also available in brilliant colours.

Chandeliers can be hung boldy from the centre of the roof or over a dining table – although cut-glass ballroom designs would not work well. Murano glass chandeliers from Venice make bold and wonderful centrepieces, particularly assembled from clear, rather than coloured, handmade and interchangeable components. A contemporary wrought-iron alternative, as illustrated opposite, can be large but is less obtrusive and may be used successfully even in a small conservatory. If you buy one with candle holders, you will need a cord and pully. Use with care so that hot wax does not drip on to people or fabrics below. The electrified version uses pretty candle-flame bulbs, but bear in mind that such lamps only contribute to the overall lighting and do not do the job alone.

Candlelight remains the most attractive light of all, with the romance of flickering flame, while large, self-supporting candles can burn for days. They will set the scene with beautiful dining table illumination if placed in pretty candlesticks or an attractive candelabra. Night lights in clear or coloured pressed-glass holders are enchanting – especially suspended along cords for a

'Use accessories with a light touch that corresponds with garden room style.'

Left: Candles make perfect lighting (although the wax can soften during a sunny day). These antique, ecclesiastical-style multiple candlesticks are useful decoration for a table in a conservatory. They can also be fixed to the framework of the building with a bracket.

Opposite: Use lots of tiny lamps with coloured shades for a party. When doors and windows are open, oil lamps are more practical than candles, unless these are in hurricane jars.

Below: Beautiful, antique, Dutch-style brass candlesticks fit well in a conservatory. The room behind is softly reflected in a *verre-eglomisé* mirror.

party. It is possible to buy good quality, scented candles with delightful real flower extract, such as stephanotis, lemon verbena and tuberose. The dazzling flicker of candlelight works well against a mirror or smooth, reflective surface, or placed to create dramatic shadows amongst the flowers and foliage in the garden room.

In shaping your lighting scheme, flexibility is all; remember that furniture and planting may need to be rearranged when plants grow larger over time, and that the original purpose and needs of the room may change. The best strategy is to fix lighting points around the room, raised 30–40 cm (a foot or so) above floor level and controlled by a switch at the entrance. It is also a good idea to plan electrical cabling for outdoor lights when first designing the room. A terrace will extend the entertaining space if cleverly lit, admitting light from outside lamps and enhancing the appearance of the conservatory behind. Waterproof lamps must be used on the external framework or masonry, designed to match the style of the garden room behind. For table illumination, hurricane lamps, deep glass containers which contain a candle protecting it from breezes, are easy to carry in and out. Citronella candles keep insects at bay and emit a lovely lemony fragrance into the evening air. For an occasion, place glass night lights around the terrace and paths for a myriad of sparkling, lights. Strings of clear or single-colour bulbs woven around balustrades, bushes and trees will extend the magic further into the garden.

Collecting

If you are by nature a collector, and have an interest in garden room antiquities, you may find yourself passionately collecting for the conservatory. I have never been able to resist old, hand-thrown flowerpots, including slim tom thumbs and perforated orchid pots, or rhubarb and seakale forcers to decorate the garden – there are now very good reproductions, but it is still nice to have the old ones. Collecting old wicker baskets is irresistible, not least because of the exquisite

workmanship, and with a lining of moss and some protection, these can be charmingly planted with bulbs. Antique wicker and cane furniture was manufactured with extraordinary variety, incorporating different weaves, textures, coloured material, even plastic and rope with curlicues, barley twists and velour upholstery. However, it does often turn out to be more fragile than it looks. Plainer, but tougher, is old Lloyd Loom, some

Far left: Thrift grows in an old terracotta pot that is shaped to sit on a windowsill.

Left: A shelf can be constructed in the gable of the conservatory above door height to be used for pots and ornaments.

of it dating back to the early years of the last century. While there are relatively few worthwhile old books specifically about conservatories or glasshouses, magnificent old catalogues and garden encyclopedias are well worth pursuing. Be careful of storing them in the conservatory, however, if it is also a plant room.

Side furniture and storage

Side tables are practical if placed at the end of sofas or at the side of loungers and armchairs, where they provide bases for table lamps. They can be made of wicker, painted wood, timber with a natural or oiled finish – oak or teak, for example – or waxed or painted steel. They look good with diagonal framing patterns reminiscent of trellis, or with slatted tops like plant staging. If plants are kept on them, a tray is practical, with gravel in the bottom if there is a group of plants. Console tables, usually about 85 cm (3 feet) high, with stone or metal tops, often fit well on a solid wall in a space between doors. They can be used for potted plants and lamps, and are convenient for serving drinks or food. The classic, half-round design looks good, and is conveniently unobtrusive.

Space for storage often presents a problem in conservatories, as they possess relatively few solid walls for tall cupboards, chests of drawers or shelf fittings. A windowsill in a recess or bay can be widened to make a broad shelf for storage and plants, and the space beneath can be infilled with doors to form a cupboard. If the sill is low enough – about 45 cm (18 in) – it can also be used as a fitted seat, but for this to be effective,

allowing room for a back cushion, it must have a depth of 70 cm (28 in). Free-standing cabinets, such as those illustrated opposite, can be placed against a wall or in the centre of the room behind a sofa, and can house a small fridge, music system, glass and china. A stone, slate or marble top will enable you to use such a cabinet for potted plants or as a surface for serving food or drinks. Low tables with shelves beneath are ideal for storing books and magazines (see page 109), while an ottoman can be brought into play to store winter or summer cushions, covers and throws.

A shallow, glazed wall cupboard with shelves painted to correspond with the overall colour scheme

Below: A garden room, with formal, drawing-room decoration towards the back, incorporates pretty bookcases that fit neatly beneath the glazed roof.

or a wire rack is good for storing china, but floor-to-roof custom-made fittings are the answer for serious storage. Where a conservatory is built against a house wall, it makes design sense to cover the wall inside with fittings that correspond with the design elements of the other sides of the room. For example, a shelving or cupboard system can follow the horizontal lines of the framework and use similar proportions. If the roof of the conservatory slopes down to the abutment with the house, there will be a box gutter 30 or 40 cm (12 or 16 in) deep, which conveniently forms the top of bookcases and cupboards.

Plant stands are unique to conservatories and are generally made of wire, steel or timber. Handsome plant staging with tiers of shelves can be positioned anywhere around the perimeter of the room. It is an opportunity for instant gardening – with groups of small plants, such as miniature roses, ferns, busy lizzies or ivy, which will quickly create an impact if arranged together *en masse*. Wirework jardinières look charming if they are painted up in pretty colours and filled with flowers. Mostly based on old French designs, they take the form of elongated baskets, quarter-round or half-round tiers or free-standing concentric baskets, forming a pyramid. I have often bought these as antiques; they can be huge, but check that the delicate wirework has not rusted through in places. Otherwise, after a coat of paint, they provide ideal decorative storage for a conservatory. Successful storage is always personal, however, relating to the ways in which the room is used from day to day.

Below: Cabinets of this type are useful: glasses and some china, a music system and even a small fridge for ice and cool drinks can be hidden inside. A practical marble top is ideal for lamps, plants and other paraphernalia, and is a good surface from which to serve refreshments.

A Room for all Seasons

Opposite: There is no reason why – with warm construction, the right colours and decoration, good lighting and, ideally, an open fire – the conservatory should not be used at night as well as during the day in the depths of winter.

Below: In winter, when the doors are rarely used, it is practical to put down a rug to make the conservatory feel and look more comfortable.

Modern improvements in insulation, combined with automatic heating and ventilation have made the conservatory into a room to live in throughout the year. The attractions of a comfortable, enclosed space that is close to the outside world yet shielded from it are undeniable, and are particularly strong in the dark winter months when our experience of the garden outside is limited. Then, in spring and summer, the conservatory opens out to become almost part of the garden, with doors and windows thrown wide to encourage a flow of activity between inside and out. More than any other room in the home, a conservatory makes the occupant acutely aware of seasonal change. The colours and the mood of the interior decoration and furnishings vary in the different lights. As a result, you only really know a conservatory – in the same way as a garden – after you have spent time in it at different times through the year.

Autumn and winter conservatories

In a room which encourages a strong awareness of the changing seasons, it is appropriate to adapt soft furnishings to the time of year. Cushions, throws and even loose covers on furniture may be changed easily. Darker, cosier winter colours and textures can be replaced by pastel shades and lightweight fabrics in spring. Rugs bring an attractive softness to hard, cold floors, are well suited to sitting areas, and can also be moved around or changed according to the time of year. Natural, textured materials for rugs include seagrass, jute, abaca (banana fibre), coir, cotton, sheep or even goats' wool, and woven or twisted paper. Light, ethnic rugs with simple patterns, such as dhurries, look good with stone, and the traditional, earthy colours of kilims blend well with terracotta flooring. In the evening, a stone or slate table can be softened in preparation for a meal with a tablecloth, perhaps of quilted cotton, wool or thick, undyed linen.

Open fires are usually associated with cosy sitting rooms rather than conservatories, but the contrast between the warmth and glow of a crackling log fire in a glass room and the grey and mist of freezing weather outside has its appeal. Fireplaces are better suited to larger conservatories, where the room can be used in zones. Comfortable wicker chairs or sofas and a rug may be placed around the fireplace, while separate dining areas, and a space for plants, are created in areas of the room close to the garden doors. It is easiest to build a fireplace if there is an existing flue in a wall against which the conservatory is built, but it cannot be used if it already serves an existing fireplace. If there is not a suitable one, a new brick or stone chimney can be built on any side of the conservatory. This will be quite large, and will become the anchor for both the design and construction of the building. An alternative, although it will still need a substantial flue, is a stove – either wood- or coal-burning. Stoves are highly efficient, and can be centrally positioned so that conservatory doors will be opened to expose a welcoming blaze.

'In the heat of summer a conservatory is the place to be – the link with the colourful and scented world of the garden outside.'

Shading and blinds

Almost all glass roofs, unless they are manufactured with costly heat-control glass (and air-conditioned in commercial buildings) will benefit from some form of shading. Most are fitted internally; although external shading should theoretically work better, because it prevents sunlight from reaching the glass, it is not always practical. A traditional external form, still manufactured on a small scale, is made from 5 mm x 20 mm (1/4 x 3/4 in-) section cedar lathes assembled into a blind with rows of copper staples. Designed to roll down from the top, these blinds only suit certain roof shapes, and the cedar gradually silvers. At an entirely different technological level are electric external, fixed blinds with aluminium vanes, which turn according to the height and intensity of the sun and close automatically in high wind. Highly effective, they are normally associated with high-tech greenhouses and glazed roofs over art galleries and atriums.

Interior blinds are protected from the weather, making the selection of their material much easier. Simple shading can be made with stretched cotton, natural flax or even sacking, but more effective materials for roofs are stiffened in some way. Traditional Holland fabric is a purpose-made, treated cotton which can be used on roller blinds. However, one of the best materials is pinoleum, developed in the nineteenth century from long pine reeds woven with a cotton warp in imitation of traditional Japanese split-bamboo blinds. Pinoleum can be made in much larger sizes than bamboo, is far more durable if woven with polyester yarn and can be stained attractively. In roofs, the blinds are usually fitted, pulling either up or down on an arrangement of taut wires with cords and pulleys. Alternatively, they may have miniature electric motors operated by a remote controller, which will open or close an entire roof of blinds in seconds. Side blinds are more a matter of style or privacy than of necessity, and allow more scope for using interesting fabrics, edgings, ribbons and ties.

Summer conservatories

With effective shades and ventilation, the summer months can be glorious in the conservatory. The long hours of daylight and higher temperatures encourage rapid plant growth and plenty of flowers. The outdoor space and the conservatory become even closer at this time of year, especially if it opens on to a terrace which becomes part of the living space until early autumn. Conservatory furniture finds its way out onto the terrace, as do plants grown too big for indoors. Daytime activity outdoors will move into the conservatory at dusk on cool evenings. During the summer, annual climbers and roses serve to blur the distinction between house and garden in a mass of foliage and flowers.

Conservatory entertaining

A conservatory is a wonderful place for entertaining at any time of year. Whether it is used as a venue for casual

Opposite: In this Chelsea Flower Show conservatory, built by Marston & Langinger, the walls were boarded with beaded and painted timber to contribute to the intimate and comfortable interior style.

Below: In summer, activity spills out from the conservatory on to the terrace. I use a collection of my own wire chairs and a table for the terrace of my Norfolk home, because they can be left out year-round – although the cushions must be stored.

Below: Glass hurricane lantern shades will protect candles from breezes on summer evenings when the doors are open. The dark green of the conservatory relates beautifully to the greens of the foliage outside.

prettily decorated china and glass that is in keeping with the relaxed atmosphere of the room. If you are lucky enough to have ripe figs, oranges or grapes growing in the conservatory, they can even be served straight from the plant. A conservatory can be great fun for children's parties. It allows for combined use with the garden for games, and it has surfaces – wicker or marble, for example – that will not suffer unduly from spills or rough play.

The quality of daylight at different times of the year will affect how much, if any, artificial light is needed during the day, but it should certainly be a feature of evening conservatory events. A well-designed lighting scheme will allow different illumination in various parts of the room. A dining table can be highlighted for a meal, and lighting around the garden doors or on the terrace outside can bring the landscape into focus as a

Right: It is hard to imagine using the house for a summer lunch when it can be taken in the conservatory – here served on a stone-top table with pretty china and cutlery.

Below: Pot plants, bulbs and cut flowers provide attractive table decorations in a garden room. Floral patterns on crockery and table linen strengthen the outdoor theme.

drinks or elaborate dinner parties, the space can be given the appropriate mood with table decorations, lighting adjustments and swift redistribution of furniture. Proximity to the garden is a major asset; food may be cooked indoors and eaten outside, or vice versa if there is a barbecue. If they are large enough, garden rooms are a good location for receptions, as guests can wander at will between the garden and the space inside. In the event of sudden rain, it is easier to move into a conservatory than a drawing room. In winter, particularly if there is frost or snow, the garden views provide an ideal accompaniment to warm drinks among the out-of-season blooms. At Christmas, the conservatory – often the highest room in the house – is the perfect place for a decorated tree. The room can be festooned with strings of clear or coloured miniature lights, candles, night lights and oil lamps, and be decorated with holly, poinsettia, red amaryllis, narcissi and early hyacinths.

In the evening, the room can be set for a special meal with a pretty floral cloth, lots of cut flowers and nighlights for each setting or large hurricane lamps. Use

beautiful backdrop. Certainly for a relaxed atmosphere, the lighting should be subtle and easy on the eyes. The addition of no more than a simple tablecloth, for example, considerably reduces the glare that might otherwise bounce off a marble or glass surface.

No matter how charming the design, dining chairs must be comfortable, with soft seat cushions and backs that give good support. And before buying the main dining table, you must decide how many it will regularly need to seat, and determine the maximum size that the available space in the conservatory can accommodate. The best shape for a table should also be considered. Round tables have the right informal feel but may not in fact suit the shape of the room; oval tables are practical, although the ends are a little awkward to use. Somehow square tables seem out of place in a garden room, and rectangular ones are often

the most practical. If you wish to seat lots of people, round tables larger than about 1.6 m (5 feet 6 in) – which seat between eight to nine – can become uncomfortable, making it difficult to converse with the person on the opposite side. In order to seat ten, a rectangular table 2.4 m (8 feet) in length is better. Where space against a wall is tight, a bench will take up less room than chairs.

If there is a sound system, it needs to be reasonably powerful because of the high volume of sound absorbed in a conservatory. This is particularly the case if there are a large number of rough hewn textures, such as wicker furniture and woven wool or rattan rugs. In summer, the sound will also spill out on to the terrace. Miniature speakers – one or two pairs – are best set up in the roof structure, and they are even available splosh-proof for use in close proximity to towering plants.

Above: The colours used here work especially well in the evening. At the end of the building, a recess was constructed to make a built-in snug and comfortable seat.

Right: This garden room prepared for a Christmas lunch party uses bright seasonal colours, a pretty tablecloth, cut flowers (as there are few conservatory plants in bloom), swags, large witches' balls, charming oil lamps and even Kurdish concertina lamps.

6

Plants and Planting

Plants are the essential ingredient inside the conservatory, contributing to its unique style, and this remains true whether the planting has simply a decorative role or if the interior is filled with a jungle of exotic plants. For gardeners, a conservatory is an exciting opportunity to grow tender new plants, and to garden comfortably indoors, all year round. For the majority of us, conservatory gardening means selecting plants that can be cultivated successfully in an environment also suitable for people (a good choice of mostly easily grown Mediterranean plants is listed in the directory on page 150). Plants set against furniture need to be well grown and look good throughout the year. Most are evergreen and should be selected for good foliage regardless of their blossom. Containers make an immense difference – just removing a plant from a cheap plastic container into a handsome, hand-thrown terracotta pot will be a huge improvement.

Opposite: Mediterranean plants are suitable for a glasshouse that is also used by people. An example is bougainvillea, which can produce masses of brightly coloured flowers for several months of the year in a sunny conservatory.

Growing under Glass

I clearly remember a winter visit to Kew Gardens as a child in the 1950s, when we took shelter in the Great Palm House after a sudden deterioration in the weather. The pleasure of stepping into a steamy, lush interior while snow settled outside was unforgettable, and I am convinced the experience contributed to a life-long interest in gardening under glass.

However, success is not always easy to achieve. I am sure most conservatory owners could admit to failed attempts with plants requiring a consistently higher winter temperature or greater humidity than is practical in a space shared with people. And no matter how much glass and heating a room has, the season outside still plays an important role. Some plants languish because the amount of sunshine is limited by the length of day in a particular area; elsewhere, a hot summer and insufficient shading may cause others to decline. Nevertheless, a wide range of interesting and decorative plants, impossible to cultivate outside, can flourish in a furnished conservatory used as a room in the home.

Although conservatory gardening presents particular challenges, it offers a unique opportunity to grow a variety of tender and exotic plants. The key is to be both realistic and imaginative in your selection, and to create a scheme of plants, like those of decorating colours and furnishings, that balances practical needs and personal taste. Provided that there is sufficient ventilation, shading and heating, and adequate levels of humidity in the atmosphere, plants can be chosen to suit any aspect and environment. Indeed, the speed of indoor growth may be a shock for the unwary – a young jasmine or vigorous passion flower, for example, can virtually cover the roof in a season, and a banana plant can grow to 3 metres (10 feet) in the same period.

Plants for a conservatory, unless it is fully devoted to horticulture, are best in free-standing containers. The room will be easier to maintain without problems of damp around built-in beds, and pots permit you to re-arrange the room to reflect changing seasons.

Left: Plants in containers can easily be adjusted to highlight those in bloom at different seasons.

Right: Camellias produce a brilliant show of flowers, but no scent, and with time grow into handsome, glossy-leafed shrubs. On the right is *Adiantum venustrum* (maidenhair fern), a useful cover plant for dark areas. However, it must be kept continuously damp.

Far left: The *Cycas* (sago palm) is a beautiful, fern-like plant which each year throws up a dramatic crown of fresh leaves. This opens into a shuttlecock of dark-green, glossy fronds, about one metre (40 in) in length.

Left: A bold riot of colour in a display of wall and roof climbers and well-filled staging supported on turned columns. Amongst the plants are *Streptocarpus* (Cape primrose), fuchsia, plumbago, *Passiflora* (passion flower), geranium, petunia and campanula.

Heating, humidity, light and shade

Modern conservatories are usually double-glazed and well insulated, offering the possibility of growing lots of plants that could not live in the garden greenhouse. Although many plants will survive in a frost-free environment, the right minimum temperature is essential if they are to thrive. Success with stephanotis, for example, is achieved by ensuring that the room is not too cool at night. If the conservatory is heated from a domestic central-heating boiler, where the house heating is turned off at night, you should either have a separate feed to the conservatory with its own controls from the boiler or you should supplement the conservatory heating. Maintaining lots of plants at high temperatures through the year is not only expensive, but may also be detrimental to furniture, fabrics, books and magazines. It is also mostly unnecessary, as many interesting and unusual plants can be grown successfully with very little heat.

Creating the right humidity is the most difficult aspect of gardening in a conservatory. Gardening guides recommend hand-spraying plants with water, mostly in the morning, but many of us do not have the time for such niceties. A good approach is to keep plants in

'Conservatories are safe havens for many exotic, tender plants. Shape, texture, fragrance and colour bring a garden room vividly to life.'

groups so that they create a micro-climate around them. This collective emission of water from leaves and soil works even better if plant pots are positioned on shallow trays of pebbles.

Even on the sunniest domestic sites, conservatories offer, at best, a partially shaded habitat. Plants requiring a semi-shaded environment should be selected, even if the conservatory is south-facing – when it will need screening from bright sun between May and August to avoid drying out and unattractive leaf scorch. A north-facing conservatory encourages leaf growth, and is good for hanging baskets of ferns and other foliage plants: a south-facing conservatory, by contrast, is more suitable for colourful blossom.

Left: Decorative cast-iron grilles are a traditional way of heating conservatories. They were used by serious gardeners for 'damping down' – watering through the grilles on to warm pipes beneath to produce clouds of steam.

Left: Unlike most greenhouses, a south-facing conservatory will be partially shaded by surrounding walls and by its framework, doors and windows.

Climbers for structure and impact

The high roofs of conservatories are marvellous for climbers, which use little floor space but can be trained across walls and up into otherwise neglected roof areas. They also adapt well to conservatory conditions – many are naturally forest plants, and so they are tolerant of the relative shade of a glasshouse. A climber should be planted in as large a container as is practical to allow future growth and to make routine watering less critical: small pots tend to dry out faster. Often the pot can be concealed behind a sofa or in a corner, and the plant then trained to the desired position. If the container is exposed, the soil around the stems can be planted with ground-cover plants: for example, wood sorrel, especially the Mexican variety *Oxalis tetraphylla*,

with its triangular, purplish leaves and small pink flowers, or *Ophiopogon planiscapus* 'Nigrescens', a low, grass-like plant with near-black leaves.

Evergreen climbers are the best option, so I would usually avoid a grapevine (except in a working greenhouse) – for five months of the year there will only be bare ropes of twisting, greyish vines. The perfect climber must be jasmine. The most commonly grown variety, *Jasminum polyanthum*, with masses of perfumed, pale pinkish flowers, is widely available from garden centres and supermarkets. Released from its ubiquitous plastic pot into a foot-square container, unravelled from its wire hoop and trained up into the roof, it will, within a year or two, produce clouds of blossom to scent the entire house.

Above: Jasmine is easy to grow and prolific. Within a couple of seasons, it produces an extensive mist of heavenly scented white blossom.

Below: *Abutilon mega-potamicum* is evergreen when grown indoors and in a large pot will reach 150 cm (5 feet), producing quantities of small, red and yellow flowers from spring to the end of the year.

There are several climbers that can be grown rapidly from seed: morning glory (*Ipomoea* sp.), with its astoundingly blue trumpet flowers, does well in a south-facing room – but do not sow it too early, or it may fail. If you seek quick results, the annual flowering vine *Cobaea scandens* can fill the room within months of sowing, and often lasts through the winter. Roses are generally best grown outdoors, but possible exceptions are the half-hardy climbers, such as *Rosa banksiae*, which has masses of creamy white flowers, and the glamorous *Rosa* 'Maréchal Niel'.

It is all too easy for climbers to let rip in the roof of the conservatory, and they do look marvellous in the first year or two when growth is still fresh. However, they should be cut back, old material removed, and the

Above: White bougainvillea is a popular hybrid alternative to the natural red and cerise-purple varieties. All need to be anchored to a support in order to climb well. They flower throughout the summer months and well into autumn.

Left: An attractive evergreen climber, the golden trumpet vine, or *Alamanda cathartica*, thrives in a warm and moist environment. Glorious yellow flowers produce distinctive vanilla fragrance, and the plant will climb vigorously if supported by wires.

stems pruned to encourage new growth. Climbers also need to be kept beneath the roof blinds, trained on taut cords or, even better, on wire. Where the conservatory is wooden-framed, this can easily be done without harming the building, using long screw eyes fitted around the eaves and at the ridge.

Trellis entwined with attractive exotic climbers is an excellent use for solid walls, especially natural brick, stone or stucco. Galvanized-wire trellis made in panels suits the scale of a conservatory, is easy to install and requires no maintenance. Purpose-made wooden trellis is better than the types on offer in garden centres, and may be painted to enhance foliage and blossom – although this requires a light touch. Climbers also grow well on frames, usually pyramidal, pressed into a pot's rim. Careful twining and tweaking can create a bold mass from several individual climbers planted beneath.

Left: Small plants may be used to cover the bare tops of larger bulbs. This wicker basket contains attractive variegated ivy to complement *Amaryllis hippeastrum*.

Opposite: Bulbs are quick to grow and rarely fail, and are often gorgeously scented. Most spring bulbs flower just when they are needed, at the end of a dark and colourless winter.

Below: Because they store food, bulbs can be grown in water without soil (although they will be blind the following year). All they need is support for their roots: shingle, coarse sand, marbles or pebbles - stylishly silvered in this instance.

Bulbs for fragrance and colour

Bulbs produce some of the most beautiful flowers, and are amongst the easiest plants to grow and bring into bloom. They adapt to difficult climatic conditions by storing food, to be released the following year in rapid growth. Bulbs can be planted up and placed on a sill or table as soon as growth begins, and they include species that are amongst the earliest of the year to flower. After flowering, if it is warm enough, bulbs and pots should be put outside in the garden soil to ensure watering. Later on, pots can be lifted and cleaned.

There are hundreds of bulbous plants to choose from in specialist mail-order catalogues. Those described below are some of the most rewarding for decoration and scent. Beware, however, of plants dug up illegally from the wild. Unfortunately, bulbs are still gathered all over the world – even snowdrop and lily-of-the-valley from our own natural woodlands.

Miniature narcissus. Paper-white varieties, with clusters of heavily scented, small flowers on 40 cm (16 in) stems and *Narcissus* 'Soleil d'Or', with its delicate, golden-yellow flowers, are amongst the easiest of all bulbs to grow. Even without soil their roots will spread through grit, pebbles, or even glass marbles in a glass container. Ensure that the water reaches up to the bottom of the bulbs.

Amaryllis. These are large, tropical bulbs, with lily-like flowers in brilliant colours. The related monster *Hippeastrum* has some varieties with bulbs weighing up to a kilo (over 2 pounds), producing four or five stems and twenty or more flowers, and a range of colours, including exotic striped varieties.

Lilies. Most garden lilies also do well in pots, offering colour, scent and shape inside or out from early summer to autumn. My favourites are those with downward-facing blooms, such as *Lilium pardalinum* – red and yellow with maroon spots – the rose-purple *Lilium martagon*, which, left undisturbed in a pot, gets better every year, and the madonna lily, *Lilium candidum*, with lots of pure white, waxy, trumpet-shaped flowers. The

variety *Lilium regale*, with white, well-scented flowers streaked purple outside, is easy to grow; tiger lilies (*Lilium tigrinum*) are tall, with spotted orange flowers; and *Lilium rubellum* has beautiful, soft pink flowers. Grow them outside in a sheltered place and bring them in to flower.

Scarborough lily. This is a bulb of the amaryllis family, which provides late summer colour. The commonest variety, *Vallota speciosa*, has bright scarlet flowers, but white, pink, or bi-coloured forms also exist.

Hyacinth. This is an exceptionally easy bulb that can be forced indoors from Christmas onwards. It needs little water at first, and must be kept in the dark until growth starts. All have heavenly scent, and the classic *Hyacinthus orientalis* 'Delft Blue' is a good, deep colour. Other varieties include white, pink, purple and mauve.

Cyclamen. A group of autumn- or spring-flowering bulbs, varieties that combine good shape with often beautiful leaves through which pink, red or white flowers uncurl are bred from *Cyclamen persicum*. Some are multi-coloured, or even have frilly petals. The smaller varieties are excellent grouped together.

Above: This attractive display of plants derives its impact from the different heights, shapes and textures of the individual containers. From well-worn terracotta pot to polished wood, smooth curved bowl to delicate iron stand, the varied levels and surfaces complement each plant's foliage and flowers.

Left: An olive grown as a standard in a terracotta pot will succeed under glass when there is plenty of light.

Plant Containers and Frames

Good containers are essential to make a decorative plant really stylish. Wire frames, hoops, pyramids and trellis are ideal for climbers and are also attractive in their own right. Wire jardinières allow groups of small plants to be combined for an instant garden.

Right: These beautiful, hand-thrown, long-tom planting pots are made of toasted clay and are available in various sizes up to 60 cm (2 feet) high.

Below: A collection of assorted antique terracotta pots decorates the floor and a cupboard top in a conservatory. The decoration on the pots includes cast, woven and swagged patterns.

Above: Trellis both supports and displays climbing plants and can be a decorative feature in its own right. It is most successful if, rather than being a standard product, it is designed for the individual space and plant. The size of the grid should be in proportion to the foliage and flowers of the climbing plant.

Directory of Conservatory Perennials

The following plants are a personal selection of perennial plants, mostly large and all suitable for a conservatory occupied by people as well as plants. I have chosen those with both interesting foliage and flowers or a wonderful scent, and included lots of climbers, all relatively easy to obtain. Obvious omissions include oleander (they really need more sun than most northern conservatories can sustain) and ferns because, much as I love them, they are more suited to a greenhouse than a garden room. I recommend supplementing a selection of the following with smaller plants, grouped together to make an instant effect – for example, elegant miniature roses, impatiens and streptocarpus. A selection of bulbs is on pages 147–8.

Most people buying plants for a conservatory for the first time, quite understandably, choose the species they like without too much concern for practical, cultural needs. The first purchase is therefore often rather hit and miss, with unexpected successes amongst the failures (spare the latter a lingering death). With experience, successful plant groupings can be built up to make the most of their appearance and the space. For example, climbers die back at the bottom as they gain height, leaving room for low-growing plants beneath. Although it is hard to resist beautiful blossom when shopping for plants, it is foliage that we live with for most of the year, and the texture and pattern of leaves, one plant against another, is most important. I have excluded a number of plants – hibiscus, for example – because their leaves and pattern of growth do not merit valuable conservatory space.

When choosing plants, keep in mind the dimensions of your conservatory, as well as the aspect, minimum temperature and humidity. Leave enough space to switch containers around, perhaps to avoid direct sun or give prominence to blossom or fruit in season.

Left: *Plumeria obtusa* is a reliably evergreen frangipani variety. Its scented, creamy white flowers have a bright yellow centre. Best suited to a tropical climate, it will also do well in a sheltered area of a conservatory, if kept well watered.

Abutilon x hybridum 'Nabob'

Bougainvillea spectabilis

Abutilon *(Malvaceae)*

Some varieties may be grown outside in free-draining soil, such as the frost-hardy *Abutilon vitifolium*. A small shrub with attractive leaves and exquisite, pale-lilac open flowers, it also thrives in a pot under glass. *A. striatum* 'Thompsonii' has interesting, mosaic-patterned green and yellow foliage and bold orange flowers for much of the year. *A.* x *hybridum* 'Nabob' has exceptional deep-red flowers.

Acacia *(Leguminosae)*

Australian trees and shrubs, some with grey-green leaves and scented yellow flowers that appear during winter and early spring, make excellent large conservatory plants. The variety *Acacia dealbata*, mimosa, has silvery leaves and clusters of golden-yellow, furry balls of flowers. It is really a tree and needs planting permanently in a conservatory border, or as a centrepiece. Two varieties that can be pot-grown are *A.baileyana* and *A. pravissima*, with curious silvery, triangular leaves.

Agapanthus *(Liliaceae)*

There are now frost-tolerant versions that can be grown outside, but the older, evergreen *Agapanthus africanus* is larger, with deep-blue flowers on 80 cm (30 in) stems and broad strap-like leaves. It provides attractive foliage inside during the winter, and can be put outside on a terrace to flower during the warm summer months.

Aloysia *(Verbenaceae)*

Aloysia triphylla is commonly known as lemon verbena. It has a tendency to become a straggly bush unless well pruned, but should nevertheless be grown for its leaves, which have a wonderful lemon scent when brushed against or crushed.

Billbergia *(Bromeliaceae)*

The exotic green, blue and pink flowers of *Billbergia nutans* appear from a mass of long, greyish leaves. It is easily grown, pest free, and requires no heat.

Bougainvillea *(Nyctaginaceae)*

These brilliantly coloured bushy climbers are a familiar Mediterranean sight. There are many varieties, single and double, pink, red and white. In the conservatory, they need a really sunny position and feeding during summer to produce masses of colour that can last well into autumn.

Camellia *(Theaceae)*

Shrubs with glossy, deep-green leaves year round and rose-like white, pink or red blooms in early spring. There are hundreds of varieties, featuring beautiful single, double or even striped flowers. Camellias are long-lived and planted in a large tub or, better still, the border of a cool greenhouse-conservatory, will grow into small trees. Though unusual, it is possible to grow *Camellia sinensis*, the tea plant, under glass.

Citrus reticulata (clementine)

Gardenia jasminoides

Citrus *(Rutaceae)*

The group that includes orange, lemon, grapefruit, madarin, clementine and calamondin, citruses can be amongst the best plants for a conservatory, with their shiny evergreen leaves, scented white flowers and colourful fruit – often all on the bush simultaneously. Select either a well-shaped bush or a standard, and plant permanently in an attractive pot. Citruses need an even temperature and prefer plenty of light; they also require careful watering and regular feeding during the growing season.

The *Citrus limon* 'Meyer' lemon is a popular hybrid, easy to grow and flowering well. *Citrus mitis* (calamondin) does particularly well in pots and produces successions of miniature oranges, which though rather sharp can be used to make delicious marmalade. Sweet orange, grapefruit, lime and mandarin can all be grown in the conservatory, but buy grafted plants rather than growing from pips.

Clivia *(Amaryllidaceae)*

Handsome plants with firm, arching, deep-green leaves, clivia produce clusters of bright orange-red flowers on fleshy stems in early spring. They can be left undisturbed for at least five years at a stretch to become potbound. Roots protruding from the surface are not a concern but indicate good humidity. It is best to shade clivia from direct summer sun, as this may bleach the foliage. Liquid fertilizer every three or four weeks in the summer ensures flowers every year.

Cobaea scandens *(Polemoniaceae)*

A rampant climber which will cover the inside of the conservatory roof in one season, and probably the outside as well, if allowed. Its bell-shaped flowers turn gradually from green to purple. Usually sold as seed to be grown as an annual, in a conservatory cobaea will flower through the following winter.

Datura (Brugmansia) *(Solanaceae)*

The shrubs from this genus, also known as *Brugmansia*, produce huge, trumpet-shaped flowers, which hang in quantity beneath the leaves. They are excellent grown as a standard plant, flowers hanging just above head height; white varieties are richly scented. *Brugmansia knightii* is an impressive, double-white variety. *Brugmansia sanguinea* has orange flowers with red tips; it can flower for most of the year. Cream, lemon and apricot-coloured varieties also exist. Easy to grow in pots, they may reach 2.5 metres (8 feet) in the ground. Every part is poisonous.

Dicksonia (*Cyathacea*)

These wonderful tree ferns resemble shuttlecocks, with enormous green fronds unfurling from a woody trunk. They need moist semi-shade and so best suit a conservatory devoted to plants, not people. True ferns, they have a single bud terminating a vertical stem. *Dicksonia antarctica*, native to south-eastern Australia, is available as a dead-looking trunk, which sprouts when planted.

Ipomoea learii

Jasminum polyanthum

Eriobotrya *(Rosaceae)*
The loquat, *Eriobotrya japonica*, will not bear fruit in a pot, but is grown as a foliage plant for its large, handsome leaves, toothed with rust-coloured hairs beneath. In a large pot, *Eriobotrya* will eventually reach the roof.

Ficus *(Moraceae)*
The large leaves of the fig create excellent foliage and, grown in the pot with its roots restrained, it will fruit well in a sunny position. Prune to a good shape. There are numerous varieties available.

Gardenia *(Rubiaceae)*
With its heavenly-scented, Jersey cream-coloured flowers amongst glossy green leaves, this plant is irresistible. To succeed and continue flowering, it needs a warm, moist atmosphere – avoid sudden drops in temperature – and so benefits from being sprayed with water as often as possible during the summer. Unless you live in a soft-water district, always use rainwater, and ericaceous compost.

Gloriosa *(Liliaceae)*
Exotic climbers grown from tubers planted in March, *Gloriosa rothschildiana* and *G. superba* have lily-like flowers with red or orange and yellow crinkly petals. *Gloriosa* climbs, supporting itself with tendrils from the tip of its leaves, to about 2 metres (6.5 feet) in a warm conservatory. They are also poisonous.

Hoya *(Asclepiadaceae)*
Among the many varieties available, *Hoya carnosa* is an attractive evergreen climber. Well suited to the conservatory, it has succulent, shiny, pointed leaves and fragrant, flesh-white flowers which hang in clusters and develop a dew of nectar. Easy to grow, it can be trained up on long wires beneath the roof so that the flowers can be seen from below.

Ipomoea *(Convolvulaceae)*
An attractive evergreen climber, morning glory is a vigorous twiner with quantities of large, trumpet-shaped flowers which each last for a day through the summer months. *Ipomoea tricolor* 'Heavenly Blue' is the fast-growing annual climber with sky-blue flowers, easily grown from seed in April, and succeeds on canes or cords over a window or on a tall frame over a pot. Other good varieties are *I. purpurea* and *I. indica*, both purplish. The *I. tricolor* varieties include blue and white striped, blue and mauvish flowers.

Jasminum *(Oleaceae)*
Ideal for the conservatory, jasmines are evergreen and easy to grow, with clouds of sweet-scented flowers from January onwards. The most easily available, *Jasminum polyanthum*, produces masses of white flowers opening from rosy-pink buds, which generally appear in late winter. it can be trained for decorative effect around a circle of wire or a cane tripod. Some jasmines prefer warmer conditions: for

Musa acuminata 'Dwarf Cavendish'

Cymbidium 'Highland Surprise'

example, the beautiful *J. sambac*, with large white flowers; and *J. azoricum*, which flowers intermittently through the year and sprawls through other plants.

Lapageria *(Liliaceae)*
An outstandingly beautiful climber, with exquisite waxy, bell-shaped, deep-pink flowers (there is also a white variety) that are produced through most of the year. However, it is not an easy plant to grow, and needs a large container with lime-free soil.

Mandevilla (Dipladenia) *(Apocynaceae)*
A vigorous South American climber for a large conservatory, where it should be trained from a container or, preferably, from a border up into the rafters. *Mandevilla laxa* (*suaveolens*) has deliciously fragrant, creamy-white, funnel-shaped flowers. M. x *amabilis* 'Alice du Pont' has deep pink buds which open into pale pink flowers with yellow centres.

Musa *(Musaceae)*
Outside a hothouse, a banana plant is unlikely to produce edible fruit, but the tree-like herbaceous plants, with their enormous leaves, give a tropical atmosphere to any conservatory. Easily available varieties that are quickly grown from small plants are *Musa ensete*, with pale, yellowish-green leaves with a reddish rib (best grown in a cool conservatory), and the small *M. acuminata* 'Dwarf Cavendish', with greyish-green leaves, which can reach fruiting size.

Orchid *(Orchidaceae)*
As most orchids in the wild grow on the branches of trees, to cultivate them is a specialist task. However, there are some which are relatively easy to grow in a conservatory. *Cymbidium* is surprisingly tough, needs little heat and plenty of air, and can be kept to flower year after year. Those grown in pots should not be overwatered; they also require a more open compost than other plants. There are countless hybrids in every colour except crimson or blue.

Palm *(Palmae)*
A large group of different genera, ranging from small Mexican parlour palms to large, mostly tropical trees.

Howea forsteriana

Cyperus papyrus

Passiflora incarnata

Easy to grow, even without heat, is *Trachycarpus fortunei*, but it will eventually become too large. *Bismarckia nobilis* has spreading, grey-green palm leaves. *Phoenix* has a slim stem, with a crown of fine, coconut palm fronds; *Howea forsteriana*, the kentia palm, is a popular choice with attractive leaves.

Papyrus *(Cyperaceae)*

This grass-related plant from the genus *Cyperus* has an impressive architectural effect. Its smooth, triangular stalks rise 2 to 3 metres (6–10 feet) and are topped by a mop of feathery leaves. Found naturally on the water's edge, it is easy to grow in a simple pot immersed in a tub of water.

Passiflora *(Passifloraceae)*

Apart from the garden species, *Passiflora caerulea*, many beautiful indoor passion flowers are becoming easy to obtain. Good choices are *P. alata*, with crimson petals and a ring of striped purple, red and white filaments; *P. incarnata*, pink with skirts of striped filaments; *P. amethystina*, with pretty three-fingered leaves; modest *P. citrina*, with delicate small yellow flowers; and *P. antioquiensis*, a tall plant with brilliant geranium-red flowers. In a conservatory *P. edulis* will develop edible passion fruit in a good year.

Pelargonium *(Geraniaceae)*

Easily grown for their scented leaves year-round

Pelargonium 'Apple Blossom Rosebud'

Pelargonium 'Chocolate Peppermint'

Plumbago auriculata 'Chessington Blue'

Stephanotis floribunda

rather than for summer blossom, this group has small, pretty flowers. Good varieties are *P.* 'Atomic Snowflake', with pink flowers and lemon verbena smell; *P.* 'Attar of Roses', rose-scented and with pink flowers; *P.* 'Chocolate Peppermint', with green leaves with brown markings and a spicy peppermint scent; *P.* 'Citronella', lemon-scented; and *P. tomentosum*. Zonal pelargoniums (plants with rounded leaves with a distinct darker 'zone') grown indoors should climb against a south-facing wall for light and support. Choose either the classic brilliant red or a mixture of red, pink and white varieties.

Plumbago (*Plumbaginaceae*)

A Mediterranean favourite, with its clusters of uniquely coloured, slightly greyish-blue, flock-like flowers that last for many weeks in summer. Although plumbago does best outside, it will grow well in a tub against a wall in the conservatory. *Plumbago auriculata* 'Chessington Blue' has deeper blue flowers than the more usual varieties and is excellent indoors. There is also a white form, *P. a.* 'Sparmannia Africana'. You will need space to accommodate this fast-growing flowering shrub, with its large, soft, light green leaves. The flowers, produced in clusters during early spring, are white with showy yellow stamens. It needs annual re-potting and cutting back each spring to control its size. Pot up the cuttings, and in one season you will have bushy plants of about a metre (3 feet) in height.

Stephanotis (*Asclepiadaceae*)

Famous for its powerful fragrance, stephanotis can be bought as a small pot plant with growth trained around a hoop throughout the year. Once unravelled and planted in a larger container in a warm, but not dry, conservatory, it will grow into a spectacular tall, evergreen, twining climber. Clusters of waxy, creamy-white flowers complement the beautiful dark foliage in summer, so long as it is protected from direct sun.

Strelitzia (*Musaceae*)

Famous for its truly exotic purple and red, bird-shaped flowers, strelitzia is also worth growing for its

Strelitzia reginae

greyish-green, palm-like leaves. Leave the plant to grow into a clump in a large tub in a sunny place, and it will respond with regular flowers.

Tetrastigma (*Vitaceae*)
A rampant tropical climber with brown, hairy branches, coiled, wiry tendrils and enormous chestnut-shaped leaves (hence its name, chestnut vine). It requires shade from strong sun in summer and humidity during periods of heat.

Thunbergia (*Acanthaceae*)
Normally sold as a garden annual, *Thunbergia alata*, black-eyed Susan, makes a good-sized conservatory twiner. The classic flowers are orange with a distinctive purple-black eye, and are also sold in mixed colours, white and yellow. Flower colour lasts through the summer, complemented by attractively pointed, heart-shaped leaves. *Thumbergia* is easy to grow and will cover a frame, set over a pot. The more glamorous *T. grandiflora* is a tall climber with masses of violet-blue flowers between spring and autumn.

Tibouchina (*Melastomataceae*)
A Brazilian evergreen, this beautiful flowering shrub has large, velvety, luminous flowers of royal purple, produced continuously for many months. It eventually reaches 3 metres (10 feet), unless it is pruned back. It benefits from being grown against a wall, where it can be supported.

Tibouchina semidecandra

Zantedeschia (*Aracae*)
The white arum or calla lily from South Africa has beautiful waxy, funnel-shaped 'flowers' (in fact, spathes surrounding the true flower) amongst glossy arrowhead leaves, 60-90 cm (2–3 feet) high. It does well in pots in the conservatory, and may even come into flower as early as Christmas. The variety *Zantedeschia aethiopica* 'Green Goddess' has bizarrely green 'flowers' with white centres. *Z. albomaculata* has creamy-white flowers and white-speckled, glossy leaves, and prefers a warmer environment. Other varieties possess delicate pink, brilliant red and bright yellow flowers.

Zantedeschia rehmannii

Zantedeschia albomaculata

Index

Author's acknowledgements

This book would not have been possible without the contribution of my wife, Susan Hirsh, who designed or located numerous furnishings and accessories and then styled many of the interiors. I would like to thank the staff of Marston & Langinger and their clients who patiently allowed me and others, especially John Heseltine, to photograph their conservatories. I appreciate the patience and support of my partner, John Buckeridge, Sara Nichols, who researched the locations for the photographs and typed the manuscript, Nigel Soper, who designed the pages, and Catherine Bradley, who organized the book.

Other acknowledgements
The Publishers would like to thank the following photographers for giving permission to reproduce their copyright material:

John Heseltine: page 10 (below); 12; 13 (above); 14; 15; 16–17; 18 (below); 20 (below); 21; 24 (above); 25; 28; 30 (above); 32–33; 34; 38; 40; 41; 44; 45; 52; 55; 56; 58; 59 (above left, centre left, below left); 60 (above and below); 61 (above right, below right); 62–63; 64 (above); 66; 68; 69 (above and below); 70 (below); 78 (above right); 79; 80 (above left and right); 86; 89 (above left); 92; 93; 95 (below); 96–97; 99; 107 (below); 110 (above right, below right); 111; 112 (above); 121 (above right); 122 (below left, below right); 123 (below); 124; 125 (above left); 126; 127 (above and below); 128 (below); 129; 134 (below); 137; 140 (above and below); 143 (above); 145 (below); 148 (above right, below); 149; 150; 151 (right); 152; 153 (left); 156 (above left and right); 157 (above).
Peter Marston: page 11; 19; 27; 29; 31; 35; 46; 47; 50; 51; 59 (centre right); 67; 71 (top right); 75 (top); 76–77; 85; 89 (bottom left); 91; 95 (top); 103; 106; 113; 116 (bottom); 120; 133; 140 (bottom); 143 (bottom); 146 (top and bottom); 148 (top left); 153 (right).
Marston & Langinger: page 2 (photographer Clive Boursnell); 6 (Christoph Koster); 9 (Christoph Koster); 13 (bottom); 18 (top); 20 (top); 21–22 (Christoph Koster); 30 (bottom: Gary Rogers); 36–37 (Christophe Koster); 39 (Gary Rogers); 42–43 (Christoph Koster); 61 (top left); 71; 74; 75 (bottom); 80 (top: Robin Matthews); (bottom: Simon Archer); 81; 83 (Robin Matthews); 84 (Robin Matthews); 87 (Christophe Koster); 89 (top right: Robin Matthews); 94 (Clive Boursnell); 100 (Christoph Koster); 101 (Christoph Koster); 102 (Robin Matthews); 109 (Christoph Koster); 114 (Gary Rogers); 115 (bottom: Gary Rogers); 116 (top left: Robin Matthews); 117 (Simon Archer); 121 (Gary Rogers); 123 (top: Robin Matthews); 127 (top: Christoph Koster); 135 (Gary Rogers); 136 (John Miller).
Deni Bown: page 139; 141; 144; 145 (above left and right); 147; 151 (left); 154; 155; 156 (below); 157 (below left and right).
Robin Matthews: page106; 118–119; 125 (above right); 131; 132 (and detail 73 above right); 142.
Fritz von der Schulenberg/Interior Archive: page 49.
Amdega Ltd: page 24 (below left); 48; 72; 130.
Bartholomew Conservatories: page 10 (above right); 57 (and detail, page 89 below right); 98; 107 (above).
Frost Conservatories Ltd (photographer C. Frost): page 73 (below left).

The Publishers would like gratefully to acknowledge the assistance of all the owners of the conservatories featured in this book and of the following conservatory manufacturers and designers:

Marston & Langinger Ltd
192 Ebury Street
London SW1W 8UP
Tel: 020 7824 8818
Fax: 020 7824 8757
Email: sales@marston-and-langinger.com

Amdega Ltd
Faverdale
Darlington
County Durham
DL3 0PW
Tel: 0800 591 523 or 01325 468522
Fax: 01325 489209
website: http://www.amdega.com

Bartholomew Conservatories
Unit 5
Haslemere Industrial Estate
Haslemere
Surrey
GU27 1DW
Tel: 01428 658771
Fax: 01428 656370
website: http://www.bartholomew-conservatories.co.uk

Frost Conservatories
and Garden Buildings Ltd
The Old Forge
Tempsford
Sandy
Bedfordshire
SG19 2AG
Tel: 01767 640808
Fax: 01767 640561
Email: sales@frostconservatories.co.uk

Sincere thanks are also due to Jim Knight at Chessington Garden Centre, Leatherhead Road, Chessington, Surrey for his help with the botanical information and plant photography in chapter 6.